Vibe Coding with GitHub Copilot

Enhancing Productivity by Leveraging GitHub Copilot Inside Visual Studio

Naga Santhosh Reddy Vootukuri

Apress®

Vibe Coding with GitHub Copilot: Enhancing Productivity by Leveraging GitHub Copilot Inside Visual Studio

Naga Santhosh Reddy Vootukuri
Seattle, WA, USA

ISBN-13 (pbk): 979-8-8688-2195-0   ISBN-13 (electronic): 979-8-8688-2196-7
https://doi.org/10.1007/979-8-8688-2196-7

Managing Director, Apress Media LLC: Welmoed Spahr
Acquisitions Editor: Smriti Srivastava
Editorial Assistant: Jessica Vakili

Cover image from Pixabay.com

Distributed to the book trade worldwide by Springer Science+Business Media New York, 1 New York Plaza, New York, NY 10004. Phone 1-800-SPRINGER, fax (201) 348-4505, e-mail orders-ny@springer-sbm.com, or visit www.springeronline.com. Apress Media, LLC is a Delaware LLC and the sole member (owner) is Springer Science + Business Media Finance Inc (SSBM Finance Inc). SSBM Finance Inc is a **Delaware** corporation.

For information on translations, please e-mail booktranslations@springernature.com; for reprint, paperback, or audio rights, please e-mail bookpermissions@springernature.com.

Apress titles may be purchased in bulk for academic, corporate, or promotional use. eBook versions and licenses are also available for most titles. For more information, reference our Print and eBook Bulk Sales web page at http://www.apress.com/bulk-sales.

Any source code or other supplementary material referenced by the author in this book is available to readers on GitHub. For more detailed information, please visit https://www.apress.com/gp/services/source-code.

If disposing of this product, please recycle the paper

Table of Contents

About the Author

Naga Santhosh Reddy Vootukuri is a Principal Software Engineering Manager at Microsoft, working within the Cloud Computing + AI (C+AI) organization. With over 18 years of experience spanning across three countries (India, China, and the United States), Naga has developed a rich and varied technical background. His expertise lies in Cloud Computing, Artificial Intelligence, distributed systems, and microservices.

At Microsoft, Naga leads the Azure SQL Database team, focusing on optimizing SQL deployment processes to enhance the efficiency and scalability of services for millions of databases globally. He is responsible for the entire infrastructure of the Azure SQL deployment space and has been instrumental in the development of Master Data Services product.

In addition to his professional roles, Naga is deeply involved in the tech community as a speaker, technical book reviewer for different publishers, and contributor to platforms like DZone and the Microsoft Tech Community. As a Senior IEEE member, Naga served as IEEE AI Summit 2024 Committee Chair in selecting some of the best lightning talks. He also delivered AI-related workshops and received an AI innovator award from Washington Senator Lisa Wellman. He is currently a Co-chair for selecting workshops for IEEE AI Summit 2025. He served as a judge for industry-wide AI/database hackathons, which further showcased his expertise and commitment to the advancement of technology. He also serves as an editorial board member for a highly reputed science journal (SCI), where he reviews research articles on Cloud Computing and AI.

Naga also actively engages in nonprofit work for the Nuevo foundation, which creates content for inspiring kids to break into the STEM world. Nuevo foundation's "Anyone Can Code" hackathon won the popular choice award in the recently conducted Microsoft 2025 Hackathon worldwide. He also mentors students and industry folks on ADPList.org and Codepath.org by conducting mock interviews and shares his experience to make a career in the tech industry. You can contact him on LinkedIn: `https://www.linkedin.com/in/naga-santhosh-reddy-vootukuri-5a67a133/`.

About the Technical Reviewer

Kasam Shaikh is a prominent figure in India's artificial intelligence landscape, holding the distinction of being one of the country's first four Microsoft Most Valuable Professionals (MVPs) in AI. Currently serving as a Senior Architect, Kasam boasts an impressive track record as an author, having authored five best-selling books dedicated to Azure and AI technologies. Beyond his writing endeavors, Kasam is recognized as a Microsoft Certified Trainer (MCT) and influential tech YouTuber (@mekasamshaikh). He also leads the largest online Azure AI community, known as DearAzure | Azure INDIA, and is a globally renowned AI speaker. His commitment to knowledge sharing extends to contributions to Microsoft Learn, where he plays a pivotal role.

Within the realm of AI, Kasam is a respected Subject Matter Expert (SME) in Generative AI for the Cloud, complementing his role as a Senior Cloud Architect. He actively promotes the adoption of No Code and Azure OpenAI solutions and possesses a strong foundation in Hybrid and Cross-Cloud practices. Kasam Shaikh's versatility and expertise make him an invaluable asset in the rapidly evolving landscape of technology, contributing significantly to the advancement of Azure and AI.

In summary, Kasam Shaikh is a multifaceted professional who excels in both technical expertise and knowledge dissemination. His contributions span writing, training, community leadership, public speaking, and architecture, establishing him as a true luminary in the world of Azure and AI. Kasam was recently awarded as the top voice in AI by LinkedIn, making him the sole exclusive Indian professional acknowledged by both Microsoft and LinkedIn for his contributions to the world of Artificial Intelligence!

Acknowledgments

I would like to thank my family for supporting me throughout this journey as it involved countless hours of work over the weekends, and they always encouraged me to pursue my dreams. Thanks to my parents (Swarnalatha Reddy and Thirupathi Reddy) and my sister (Jeevana Jyothi Reddy). Grateful to my wonderful wife Sandhya and much love to my kids (Sky Reddy and Rio Reddy). My team (SQL deployment) and my managers (Brian Chamberlain and Mohamed El Hassouni) at Microsoft encouraged and supported me when I told them about my book-writing journey. I also extend my deepest gratitude and thanks to the following:

- **Smriti and the Apress team**: I sincerely thank each one of you for giving me wonderful opportunities to work with you and with Apress. I have been an active member of the Apress technical reviewing team, and after talking to Smriti, she encouraged and pushed to pitch in the idea to pursue my book-writing journey, and this is my second book with Apress after the *Exploring Azure Container Apps* book. I will continue to write more in the future and create high-quality books.

- **Shobana**: Thanks for your support in making sure I complete my work on time and for the production support in creating Online ISBN links. It was great working with you, and I hope we collaborate more in the future.

Lastly, I would like to thank all the people from the Visual Studio and GitHub Copilot community who purchased this book and are reading this page. I hope this book will play a key role in your learning journey of exploring GitHub Copilot that you will use as a key tool for converting your awesome ideas into production-ready applications.

Introduction

If you are reading this page, I welcome you to my new book which I thoroughly enjoyed writing, and this time it's about **Vibe coding with GitHub Copilot**. I am excited that you're reading it, and I hope you will find it useful. In this book, let's explore the term Vibe coding and get started with GitHub Copilot and how it will make your life easier. It doesn't matter if you are a developer or not, this book will unfold all the tips and tricks you need to know, which makes it easier to work with GitHub Copilot so that even a nondeveloper can also put their thoughts into production-ready code.

Imagine this scenario, you're working on an important project and trying to implement a complex algorithm at 2AM and been wrestling with it for hours. You know what exactly you want to code but translating your mental model to clean code feels like climbing Mount Everest. Does it sound familiar?

How does it sound like having a coding partner who never gets tired and has memorized millions of code patterns and can understand what your goals are just by reading your comments? A partner who doesn't judge your abilities and never gets frustrated when you ask loads of questions or change the requirements at the last minute, yet patiently answers and gives you helpful suggestions. This isn't a science fiction novel – this is the current reality you are living in and the answer to it is GitHub Copilot, which is already revolutionizing the way you write code.

As we explore GitHub Copilot (GHC) throughout this book, we will dive deeper into its capabilities, limitations, and best practices on how to integrate it into your existing development workflow. The goal isn't to replace your skills as a developer but to allow you to work more efficiently, explore more possibilities, and ultimately enjoy the coding process. Gone are the days of peer programming; now we are in the world of Vibe coding, and this book will help in getting upto speed on how to utilize GitHub Copilot, which can save significant amounts of your time during coding. As always, it's your responsibility to make sure to verify the AI-generated code before consuming it in the production environment to avoid any consequences.

Throughout this book, we'll dive deep into various features of GitHub Copilot, starting from setting up on your local environment and progressing to more advanced topics of MCP and GitHub coding agents. Each chapter provides a blend of theoretical knowledge and practical demonstrations, ensuring you not only understand the concepts but also know how to apply them in real-world scenarios. Let's look at what each chapter has in store for you.

Chapter Overviews

- **Chapter 1 – Getting Started with GitHub Copilot:** This chapter lays the foundation by introducing the concept of "Vibe Coding" and GitHub Copilot as a revolutionary AI-powered development tool. We'll explore GitHub Copilot's architecture, various subscription plans, and the need for AI assistance in modern development workflows. You'll learn step-by-step instructions to set up development environments for both Visual Studio 2022 and Visual Studio Code, including authentication setup and initial configuration.

- **Chapter 2 – Exploring GitHub Copilot Features**: This chapter dives deep into GitHub Copilot's core functionality within the IDE environment. We'll explore inline code suggestions, intelligent auto-completions, and context-aware code generations. You'll master the art of crafting effective prompts through comments, method signatures, and partial code snippets to generate meaningful AI code suggestions. We also emphasize best practices for accepting, rejecting, and iterating on AI-generated code suggestions.

- **Chapter 3 – GitHub Copilot Chat in Developer Workflow:** This chapter transforms GitHub Copilot from a passive suggestion tool into an active coding companion through Conversational interfaces. We'll explore the GitHub Copilot interactive chat user interface, including Ask mode for explanatory interactions and Agent mode for autonomous multistep tasks. This chapter also demonstrates real-world scenarios from debugging complex LINQ queries to refactoring codebases following SOLID principles.

- **Chapter 4 – GitHub Copilot on the Web:** This chapter showcases GitHub Copilot's powerful web-based capabilities directly through the GitHub.com user interface. You'll learn to leverage the GitHub Copilot dashboard for repository analysis, intelligent project management, and automated pull request generation. The chapter covers daily workflows about creating GitHub issues, managing pull requests, performing code reviews, and generating extensive documentation without leaving your web browser.

- **Chapter 5 – Exploring MCP and GitHub Copilot Coding Agent:** This chapter introduces the revolutionary Model Context Protocol (MCP) and the need in using it along with creating a new MCP server using C# from scratch. We'll explore GitHub MCP server and the usage of its toolsets in real-world scenarios. We'll also cover GitHub Coding Agents with practical implementation. This chapter also covers security considerations when leveraging MCP.

- **Chapter 6 – Exploring New Features from GitHub Copilot:** It's hard to keep up with the pace of GitHub Copilot releases; however, in this chapter, we will quickly explore the recent new releases from GitHub Copilot including new GitHub Copilot CLI and also GitHub Spark in developing a production-ready application. We'll end with details about how to build on top of this knowledge and resources to keep track of new feature releases from GitHub Copilot.

By the end of this book, you'll have a solid understanding of how to leverage GitHub Copilot within Visual Studio for your daily coding tasks. You will also appreciate the power of MCP and GitHub Coding agents, which will significantly improve your developer productivity by helping you with your mundane tasks. This knowledge will help you in confidently vibe coding with GitHub Copilot to convert your awesome ideas into production-ready applications within no time. I am sure you will enjoy this pocket guide as much as I did writing it. I hope to see you with another book in the future. Until then, happy Vibe coding!!

CHAPTER 1

Getting Started with GitHub Copilot

The rate at which software development is going through a transformation is unbelievable thanks to Artificial Intelligence, which has emerged as a transformative force in how we approach coding tasks. GitHub Copilot (GHC) stands as a revolutionary tool that changes the way developers write code today, and this book is all about giving you enough tips and tricks to confidently include GitHub Copilot (GHC) in your arsenal. Regardless of your development background, this book is tailored to offer you foundational knowledge and help you with onboarding to GitHub Copilot. Buckle up and enjoy reading it!

The major difference between GitHub Copilot (GHC) from other traditional code completion tools is its ability to understand the context and generate meaningful and relevant code suggestions. Copilot can generate entire functions, classes, or even complete algorithms based on comments from the user. It's like doing peer programming except that instead of working with a human you are dealing with large language models (LLM).

In this chapter, we will embark on a journey that will transform how you think about coding. We will explore what makes GHC powerful and how to set it up to start coding with AI assistance in both Visual Studio and Visual Studio Code. By the end of this chapter, you will have a fully configured development environment and foundational knowledge to start leveraging AI in your daily coding activities.

The learning objectives for this chapter include the following:

- Introduction to Vibe Coding

- Introduction to GitHub Copilot and its offerings

- Need for GitHub Copilot in your IDE (VS/VSC)

- Pricing models and subscription options

- Step by step installation guide to set up GitHub Copilot

© Naga Santhosh Reddy Vootukuri 2025
N. S. Reddy Vootukuri, *Vibe Coding with GitHub Copilot*, https://doi.org/10.1007/979-8-8688-2196-7_1

Note   If you haven't read the introduction page, I highly advise you to read it to understand the intent of this book.

Introduction to Vibe Coding

Imagine this scenario: you are working on a complex algorithm middle of the night and stuck with an issue where you are the only one still awake in your time zone; the rest of the team logged off hours ago. In your head, you can see how this should work; however, translating that into a clean working code feels like a challenge. You could have taken your peers' help (known as Pair Programming), but now you are left with something called "**Vibe Coding.**"

Vibe Coding is an AI-assisted way of building software where a developer describes their intent in plain English and guides AI to generate and refine working code.

The term "**Vibe Coding**" was casually introduced by **Andrej Karpathy**, former researcher at OpenAI, on a post on X (formerly Twitter); refer to Figure 1-1 for the full post.

Figure 1-1. Andrej Karpathy's post talking about Vibe Coding

This post went viral and got wide attention within the industry. Vibe Coding is all about finding the perfect harmony between you and your AI assistant to create reliable software in no time.

POINT TO NOTE

*From Wikipedia, Vibe coding is an artificial intelligence–assisted software development style popularized by **Andrej karpathy** in February 2025. The term was then listed in Merriam-Webster Dictionary the following month as a "slang & trending" term.*

Introduction to GitHub Copilot

GitHub Copilot is an AI-powered tool that helps developers with coding best practices and provides auto-completion recommendations to improve overall code quality. It can produce code snippets based on the provided query. It works with a variety of programming languages and integrates well with both Visual Studio Code and Visual Studio IDE. As a developer, we can leverage Copilot to write repetitive tasks, so that you can utilize your time in implementing core algorithms and improving your development cycles. Copilot also has a chat feature where you can ask questions in your code and ask it to do mundane tasks like "Adding XML documentation to classes/methods, explaining the selected code, providing suggestions on writing tests, etc."

GitHub Copilot is launched as a technical preview in 2021 and made generally available in 2022. It's a collaboration between GitHub and OpenAI. Copilot is powered by OpenAI Codex model which is a descendant of GPT (Generative Pre-Trained Transformer) models, which were trained on billions of lines of code from public GitHub repositories.

GitHub Copilot Plans for Individuals and Enterprises

GitHub offers several plans; depending on your needs, you can either choose individual plan or as part of an organization. Refer to Table 1-1 for more details.

Table 1-1. *Comparison of various Copilot Plans*

Plan	Who it's for	Price	Core features
Copilot Free	Individuals evaluating Copilot	Free	Real-time code suggestions in supported IDEs; basic chat quota
Copilot Pro	Individual developers	$10/month or $100/year	Unlimited code completions; unlimited chat with included models; inline chat; IDE integrations (VS/VS Code/others)
Copilot Pro+	Power users/creators	$39/month or $390/year	Everything in Pro; priority/early access to advanced capabilities
Copilot Business	Teams and organizations	$19/user/month	Everything in Pro per seat; org policy controls; centralized billing; privacy-first defaults
Copilot Enterprise	Large/regulated organizations	$39/user/month	Everything in Business plus enterprise-grade identity, audit, analytics/telemetry

Need for GitHub Copilot in Your IDE

Within the field of artificial intelligence (AI), GenAI is a subset of deep learning methods that can work with both structured and unstructured data. Figure 1-2 presents the different layers of artificial intelligence.

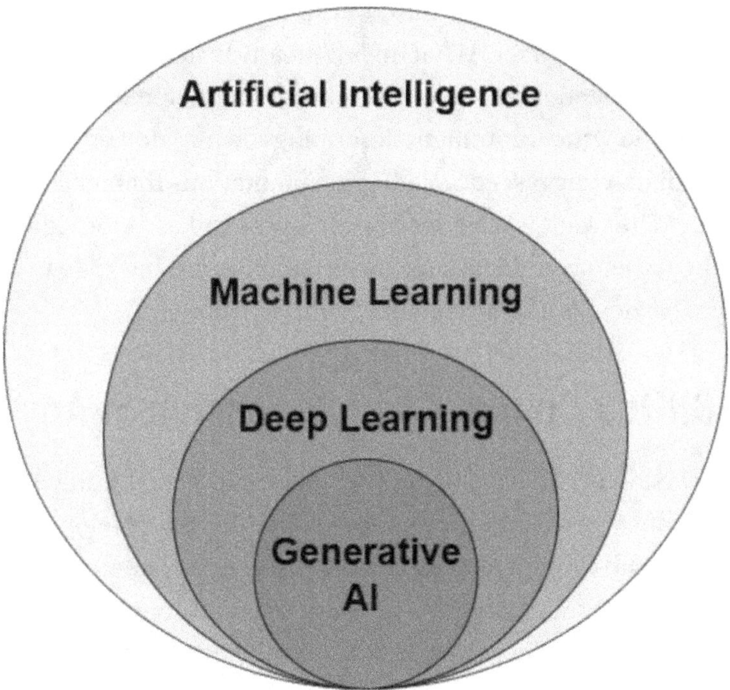

Figure 1-2. *Artificial intelligence landscape*

It is notably generative AI that is rapidly transforming the business world by fundamentally reshaping how businesses automate tasks, enhance customer interactions, optimize operations, and drive innovation. Companies are embracing AI solutions to have a competitive edge, streamline workflows, and unlock new business opportunities.

As AI becomes more woven into society, its economic impact will be significant, and organizations are already starting to understand its full potential.

In the context of software development, this AI transformation is even more impactful. Imagine on a typical day, you are constantly juggling syntax between different programming languages, making sure code doesn't have any syntax issues, writing API documentation, and switching between multiple tools and browser tabs. All this is exhausting and puts your focus away from what really matters, which is solving interesting problems and designing great software. GitHub Copilot changes all of this by bringing intelligent assistant directly into your code editor. It turns your normal IDE into a smart coding companion that understands the context and helps you with meaningful suggestions.

The integration of GitHub Copilot into your IDE makes a transition from reactive to proactive development assistance. What does it mean? Instead of waiting for you to get stuck, GitHub Copilot watches what you are doing and anticipates what you need next. For example, when you write a comment describing the function you want to create, Copilot will immediately suggest complete implementations that match your project style and structure. The result is what many developers call as "Vibe Coding" – that smooth experience where your ideas are converted into working code without getting lost in the syntactical details and implementation.

Installing GitHub Copilot As an Extension in Any IDE

While the initial version of GitHub Copilot was specific to Visual studio IDE, Microsoft has taken a significant step to its commitment to open source development by announcing that GitHub Copilot chat extension is now open source under the MIT license. This will increase transparency and foster community-wide contributions. Copilot is no longer just a tool; it's a dynamic and collaborative entity that learns and improves with community involvement.

GitHub Copilot can now be run as an extension in multiple IDEs like

    a.   JetBrains IDEs like PyCharm, WebStorm, Rider, etc.

    b.   Visual Studio

    c.   Visual Studio Code

    d.   Sublime Text (via extensions)

    e.   Vim (with plugin support)

    f.   Emacs (with copilot packages)

    g.   GitHub Codespaces

POINT TO NOTE

Throughout this book, we will use Visual Studio/Visual Studio Code as the main IDE when explaining about various functions of GitHub Copilot. However, you can get similar experience when working with other IDEs.

Installing GitHub Copilot in Visual Studio

Download and install Visual Studio 2022 IDE with version 17.6 or later by navigating to the following page:

`https://visualstudio.microsoft.com/downloads/`

Launch visual studio Installer, and on the installation page, select any workload based on your needs. Select GitHub Copilot from the list of Optional components as shown in Figure 1-3. Click next to follow prompts to install Visual studio along with GitHub Copilot extension. This contains both GitHub Copilot and GitHub Copilot Chat when installed.

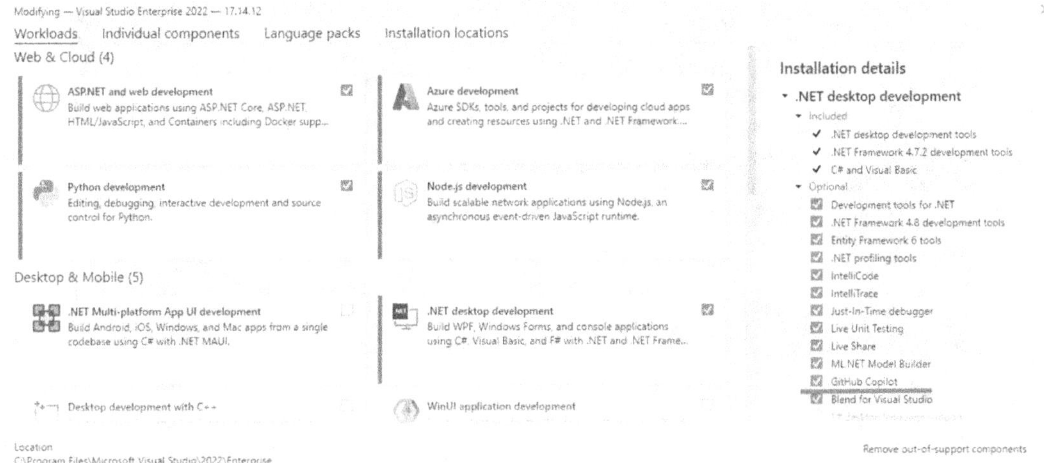

Figure 1-3. *Visual studio Installer with GitHub Copilot selected in the optional components*

It's worth mentioning that these two tools serve different purposes; GitHub Copilot focuses on assisting with code suggestions within the IDE, while GitHub Copilot Chat offers a conversational interface to help with coding tasks and provide explanations.

Now that you Installed Visual studio with an extension, other prerequisites are

    a. **GitHub Account**: Make sure to have a valid GitHub Account. Navigate to the URL `https://github.com/` to create an account before getting started.

b. **GitHub Copilot Subscription**: Navigate to the URL `https://
    github.com/features/copilot/plans` to choose a subscription.
    Plans are available for both individuals and for businesses. There
    is also a free version available for us to get started as shown in
    Figure 1-4.

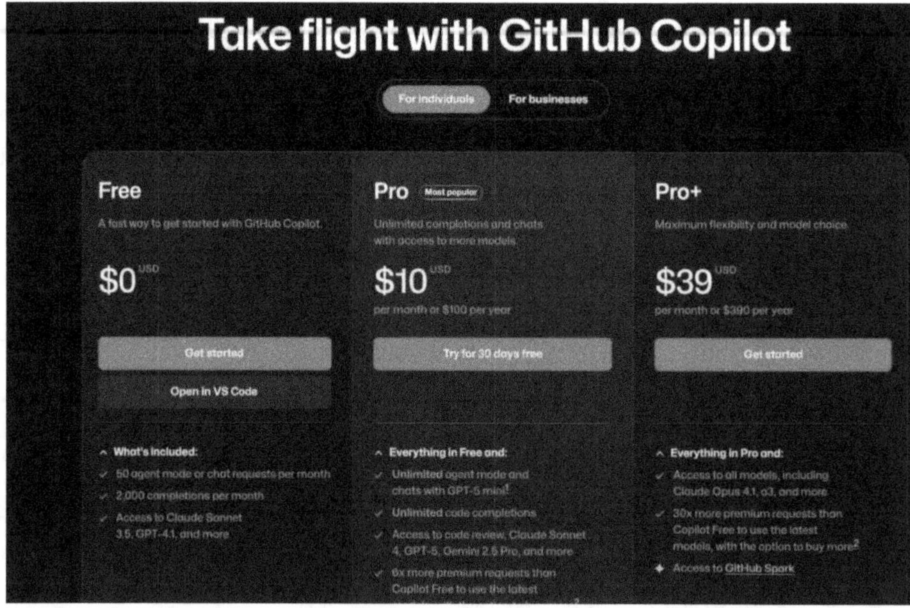

Figure 1-4. *GitHub Copilot available plans for individuals and businesses*

Once installed, you can see GitHub Copilot on the top-right corner as shown in
Figure 1-5.

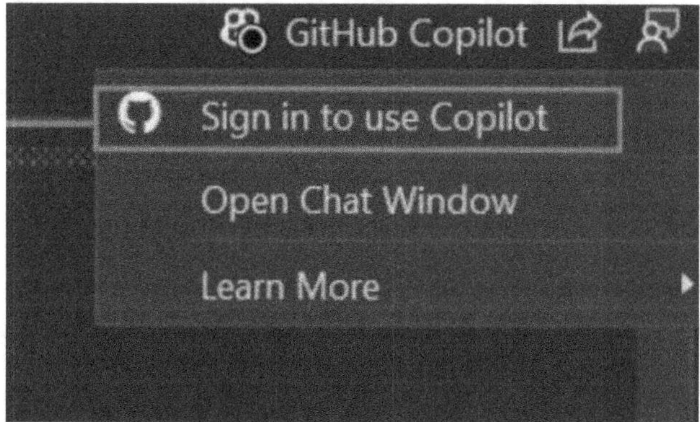

Figure 1-5. *Sign-in option available inside GitHub Copilot menu*

Make sure to sign into your GitHub Account you created in the previous step.

Once signed in with active valid account, you will see GitHub Copilot in Active mode as shown in Figure 1-6.

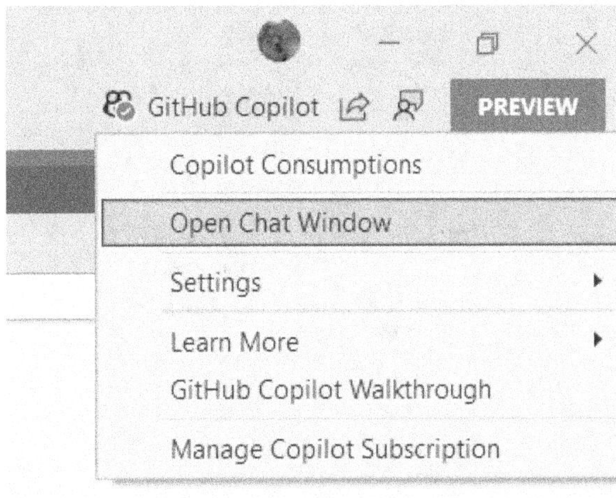

Figure 1-6. *GitHub Copilot in active mode*

You will also see a notification at the bottom-left corner that says, "Successfully authorized GitHub Copilot" as shown in Figure 1-7.

Figure 1-7. *Successfully authorized GitHub Copilot notification message*

Click on settings option to explore Copilot Chat and Copilot Completions settings in the editor to let GitHub Copilot to provide "Next Edit suggestions", and "Copilot Completions", and then you can select "Copilot completion model" as shown in Figure 1-8.

POINT TO NOTE

At the time of writing this book, for Copilot Completions Model, **GPT -4.1 Copilot August Candidate** *(preview) was available, and it was selected as shown in Figure 1-8.*

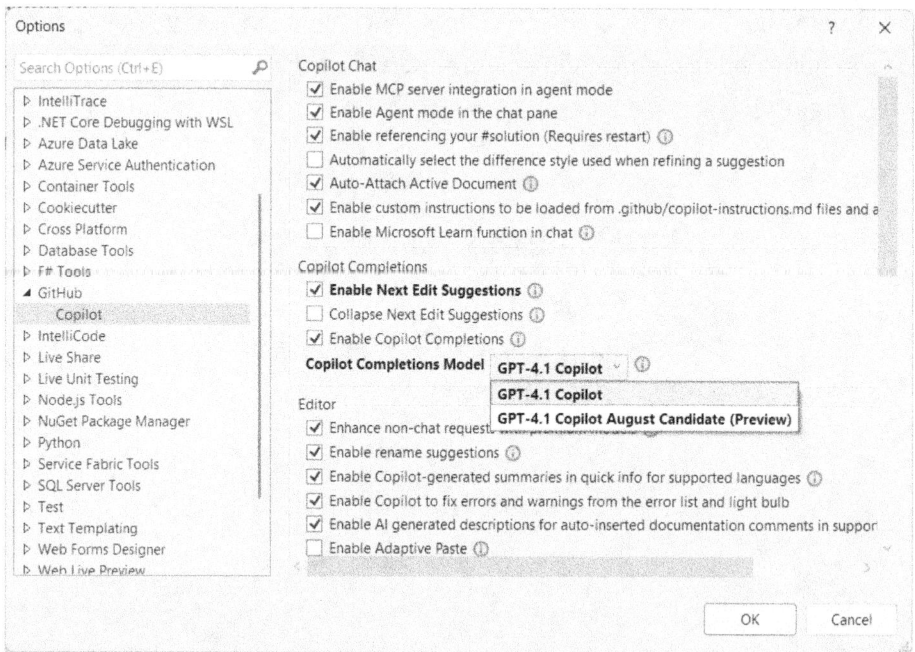

Figure 1-8. *GitHub Copilot Settings window*

For first-time users, GitHub Copilot also provides a walkthrough page, which you can select from the GitHub Copilot menu as shown in Figure 1-9.

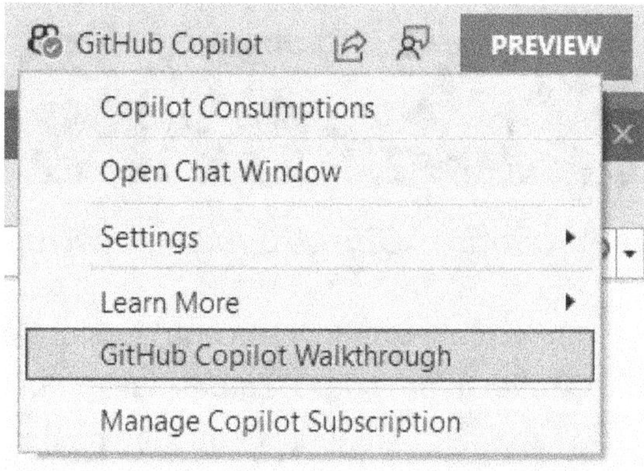

Figure 1-9. *GitHub Copilot Walkthrough option from the dropdown menu*

It then opens the Walkthrough page, which will help you get started with some of the features of GitHub Copilot as shown in Figure 1-10.

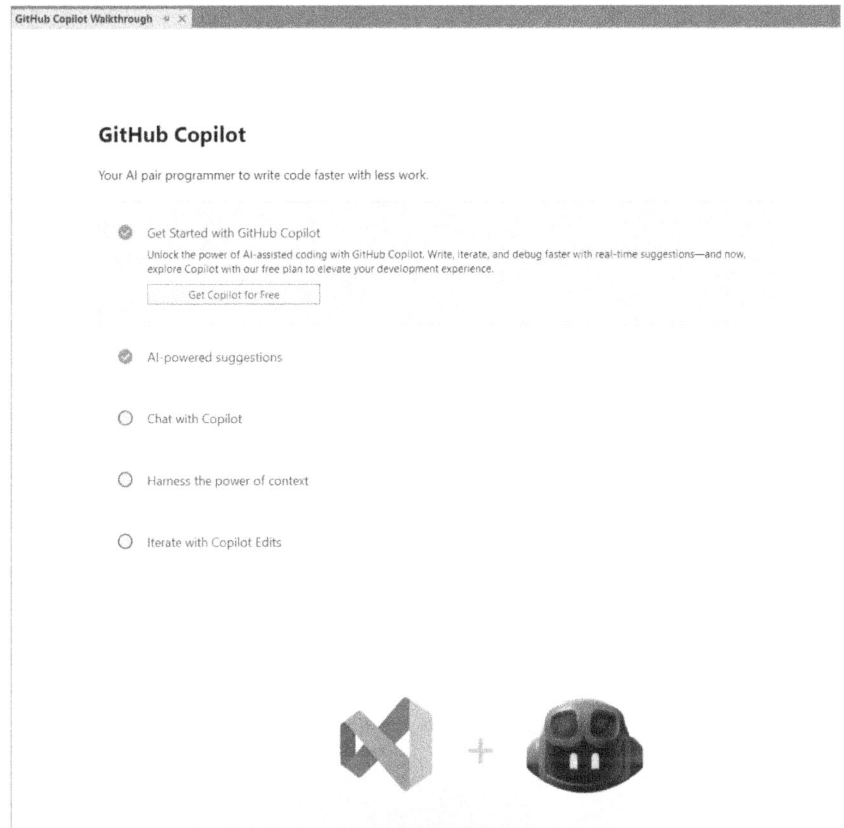

Figure 1-10. *GitHub Copilot Walkthrough page to get started*

Click on "Open Chat Window" option to open Copilot Chat window as shown in Figure 1-11, where you can communicate with Copilot asking to summarize code, write unit tests, or even fix your code by taking suggestions for improvements.

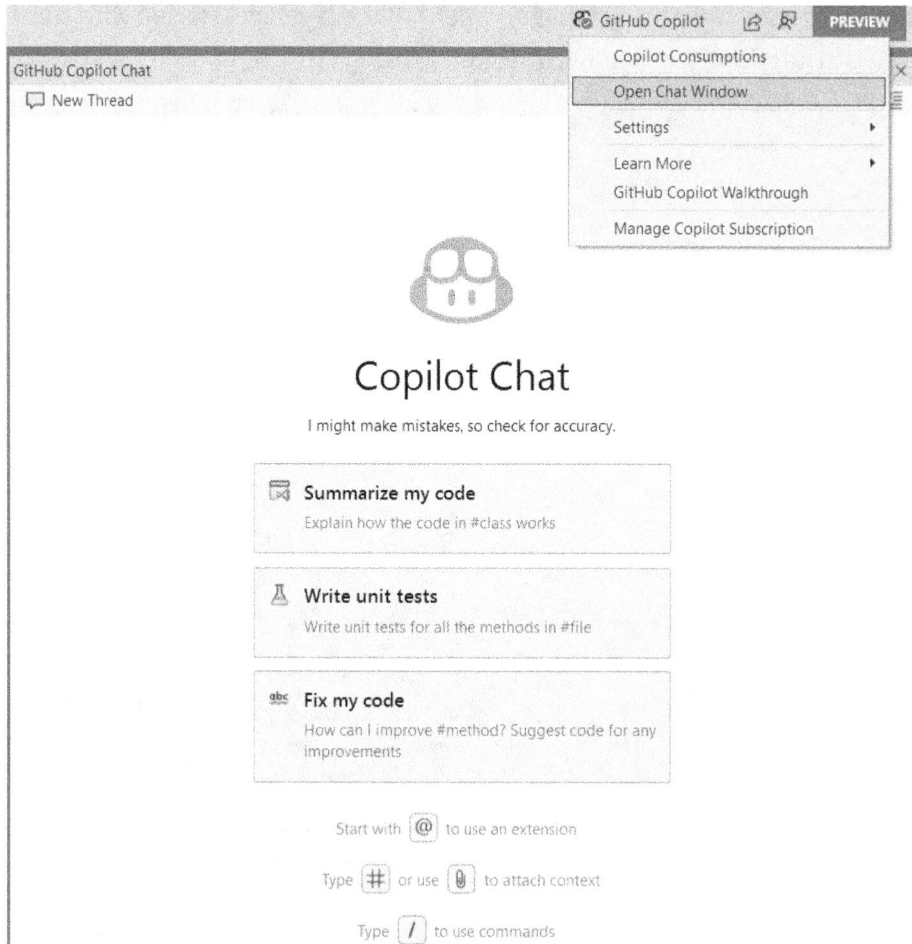

Figure 1-11. *Opening Copilot Chat window to interact with Copilot*

You can also disable Copilot any time you want by unselecting the enable option globally or for this solution as shown in Figure 1-12.

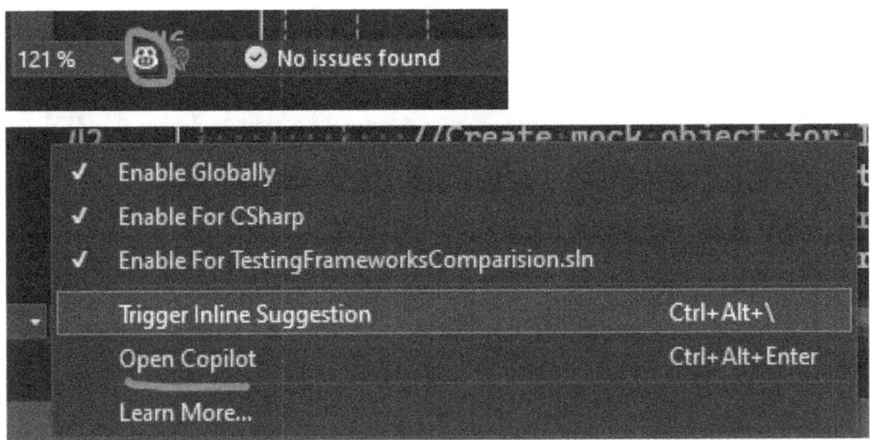

Figure 1-12. *Enable/Disable option for globally or for this solution*

Installing GitHub Copilot in Visual Studio Code

Download and install Visual Studio code by navigating to the URL `https://code.visualstudio.com/download`.

After you have set up all the requirements and gained access to the GitHub Copilot subscription, open the Visual Studio Code IDE (integrated development environments). Next, click on Extensions. Search for GitHub Copilot to install both GitHub Copilot and GitHub Copilot Chat extensions as shown in Figure 1-13.

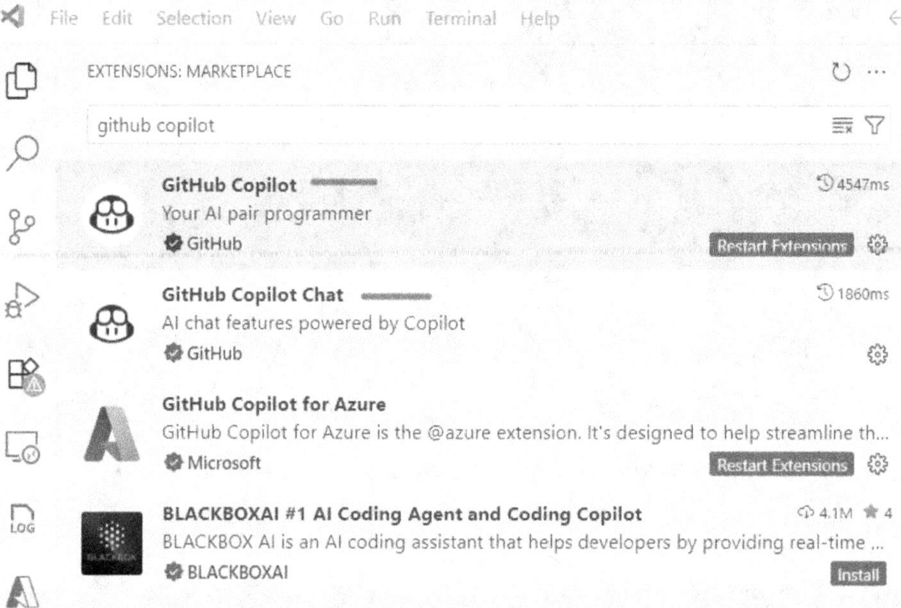

Figure 1-13. *GitHub Copilot and GitHub Copilot Chat extensions*

Once you have installed them, you will see GitHub Copilot icon appear on the top next to search bar as shown in Figure 1-14.

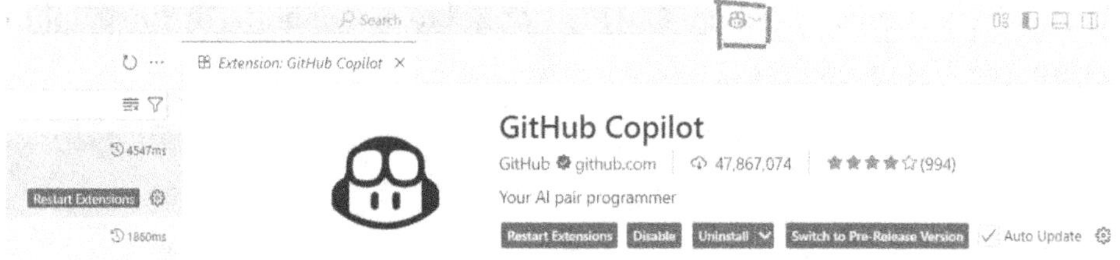

Figure 1-14. *GitHub Copilot Icon next to search bar*

GitHub Copilot chat window opens as a new Pane that can be docked to any frame in VS IDE. I generally prefer the left side, as on the right side I keep my solution explorer.

At the bottom-right corner, you can also view copilot usage statistics along with snooze option to hide Copilot Completions as shown in Figure 1-15.

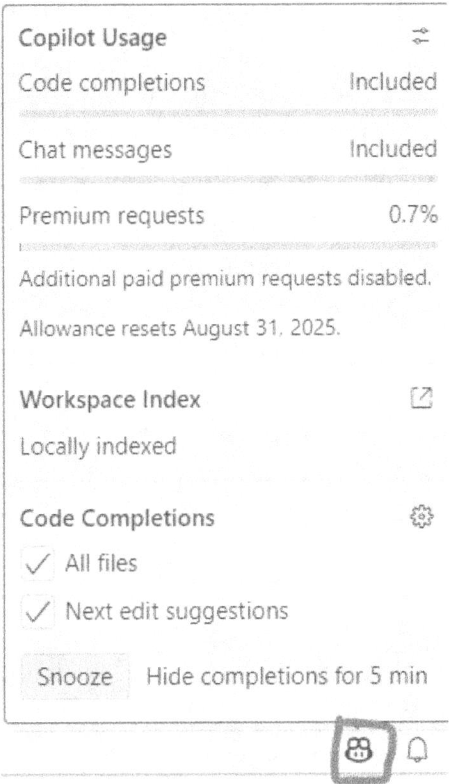

Figure 1-15. *Copilot Usage along with snooze option to hide completions by clicking bottom-right corner GitHub Copilot icon*

Q&A Session

Q1.1 What is vibe coding?

Vibe coding is an AI-assisted software development style programming where developers describe their intent in natural language and AI generates and refines the code accordingly. The term was coined by Andrej Karpathy, a former Open AI researcher.

Q1.2 What is the underlying AI model that powers GitHub Copilot?

GitHub Copilot is powered by the **Open AI codex model**. Which is a descendant of GPT (Generative Pre-Trained Transformer) models. Codex was trained on billions of lines of code from public GitHub repositories.

Q1.3 What is the main difference between "GitHub Copilot Completions" and "GitHub Copilot Chat"?

GitHub Copilot Completions provide real-time, inline code suggestions and auto completions as you type in your IDE.

GitHub Copilot Chat, on the other hand, is a conversational interface where you can ask questions to interact with CoPilot. You can ask more complex questions like code explanations, generating unit tests, and refactoring code.

Q1.4 How many GitHub Copilot Plans are available?

There are five different plans available. Copilot Free gives basic access. Pro ($10/month) offers unlimited completions for individuals. Pro_ ($39/month) adds priority access for power users. Business ($19/user/month) and Enterprise ($39/user/month) plans add team controls, security, and advanced features for organizations.

Summary

In this chapter, we explored what Vibe Coding is and how it is gaining popularity in the software industry. We also introduced the importance of GitHub Copilot as a transformational tool, and how it's changing the developmental landscape. We also discussed the process of setting up your development environment by installing GitHub Copilot and Copilot Chat extensions within both Visual Studio 2022 and Visual Studio Code. We explored and compared various GitHub Copilot subscription plans available for individuals and businesses. This chapter also discussed how to authorize Copilot, open the chat window using different methods, and manage the placement of panes for optimal workflow.

In the next chapter, we will delve deeper into practical use cases and advanced features of GitHub Copilot to enhance your coding productivity. Continue reading for more hands-on guidance and tips to use in your day-to-day coding activities.

CHAPTER 2

Exploring GitHub Copilot Features

In Chapter 1, we laid the foundation by understanding what GitHub Copilot is, the various subscription plans, and how to set up your development environment by installing both GitHub Copilot and GitHub Copilot Chat extensions. In this chapter, you will be introduced to the features of GitHub Copilot, mastering the art of prompts, and exploring advanced capabilities for documentation, code review, and asking code-specific questions. The learning objectives for this chapter include the following:

- Exploring various GitHub Copilot features like inline edits, suggestions, etc.

- How to ask relevant questions with effective prompts

- Exploring Copilot features for generating code documentation

- How to ask code specific questions using "Ask Copilot"

- Exploring real-world examples to illustrate the power of GitHub Copilot

By the end of this chapter, you will become proficient in using GitHub Copilot in your day-to-day coding tasks. You will enhance your overall productivity by writing cleaner code within Visual Studio IDE. Let's dive in!

© Naga Santhosh Reddy Vootukuri 2025
N. S. Reddy Vootukuri, *Vibe Coding with GitHub Copilot*, https://doi.org/10.1007/979-8-8688-2196-7_2

POINT TO NOTE

As with any AI tools, make sure to thoroughly review the code generated by AI before using it in production environment. LLMs (large language models) can sometimes produce inaccurate or misleading results (known as Hallucination). As a developer, it's your responsibility to always review, test, and validate AI-generated code to ensure safety and reliability.

GitHub Copilot Core Features

GitHub Copilot acts as an intelligent assistant offering you with suggestions and completions directly into your code editor by transforming your IDE into a smart coding companion. The power of GitHub Copilot lies in its ability to understand the context and help you with meaningful and relevant code snippets, suggestions, or even entire methods as you type. Let's explore some of the key features in this section.

Inline Code Suggestions

The most frequently used feature of GitHub Copilot is Inline code suggestions. Imagine you are working on an algorithm; how helpful it will be if Copilot predicts what you intend to write next? It sounds like magic; well, that's Inline code suggestions for you.

How does it work? As I mentioned before, Copilot is trained on millions of lines of code from public GitHub repositories and is fully aware of the current context; it watches as you begin to type and then it analyzes your existing code, comments, and provides you with suggestions. These suggestions appear as greyed-out text within your IDE. Copilot doesn't enforce these code suggestions onto your editor. If you think these suggestions don't meet your requirements, you can simply ignore them.

Accepting suggestions: To accept a suggestion, press the **Tab** key.

Rejecting suggestions: To ignore a suggestion, press the **Esc** key to dismiss it.

Why does it matter? GitHub Copilot's real-time assistance helps in reducing the need for boilerplate code or repetitive typing. It also helps with relevant suggestions to improve your coding patterns as per your project needs. It even discovers new APIs or new language constructs you might not be familiar with.

What triggers suggestions? Suggestions are automatically triggered by

- **Comments**: Provide your intent through comments written in natural language.

- **Method signatures**: As you start writing a method signature, Copilot can understand the context and provide you with the code implementation as suggestions.

- **Code context**: Copilot analyzes surrounding code in the file and offers you some meaningful suggestions/improvements.

Let's look at an example to understand better.

Demonstration 1

Consider you want to create a **Calculator** class with methods for calculating additions, subtraction, multiplication, and division. Without Copilot, you would type out each method's signature and body; however, with Copilot, the process becomes much faster.

Let the Copilot know your intent by adding a comment:

```
// This class provides basic arithmetic operations.
Public class Calculator
{

 // Method to add two numbers
```

As soon as you type the comment "// Method to add two numbers", Copilot will suggest you with entire method body, including parameters and return type as shown in Figure 2-1.

Figure 2-1. *GitHub Copilot giving inline code suggestions*

Not just addition, if you change the comment to *"Methods to provide basic arithmetic Operations"* or simply update the class with the comment *"A simple Calculator class with basic arithmetic operations"*, GitHub Copilot will suggest other methods too as shown in Figure 2-2.

```
// A simple Calculator class with basic arithmetic operations
0 references
public class Calculator
{
            // Method to add two numbers
        public int Add(int a, int b)
        {
            return a + b;
        }

        // Method to subtract two numbers
        public int Subtract(int a, int b)
        {
            return a - b;
        }

        // Method to multiply two numbers
        public int Multiply(int a, int b)
        {
            return a * b;
        }

        // Method to divide two numbers
        public int Divide(int a, int b)
        {
            if (b == 0)
            {
                throw new DivideByZeroException("Division by zero is not allowed.");
            }
            return a / b;
        }
}
}
```

Figure 2-2. *GitHub Copilot giving code suggestions for all methods in the calculator class*

The entire code will look like below.

```
// A simple Calculator class with basic arithmetic operations
public class Calculator
{
    // Method to add two integers
    public int Add(int a, int b)
    {
        return a + b;
    }
```

```csharp
    // Method to subtract two integers
    public int Subtract(int a, int b)
    {
        return a - b;
    }
    // Method to multiply two integers
    public int Multiply(int a, int b)
    {
        return a * b;
    }
    // Method to divide two integers
    public double Divide(int a, int b)
    {
        if (b == 0)
        {
            throw new DivideByZeroException("Denominator cannot be zero.");
        }
        return (double)a / b;
    }
}
```

POINT TO NOTE

If you look at the code carefully, especially the Divide method, Copilot is smart enough to add a condition to check for Divide by Zero exception without any prompt from the user.

Intelligent Code Autocompletions

GitHub Copilot suggests code completions as you type. For instance, when working with C# LINQ queries, Copilot can generate code automatically to simplify your work.

Figure 2-3 shows how Copilot can understand the context by looking at your code and offers you with autocompletions. Press the Tab button to accept or Esc button to ignore it and continue typing.

```
        0 references
✓ ····internal·class·Program
  ····{
            0 references
✓ ········static·void·Main(string[]·args)
  ········{
  ············var·numbers·=·new·List<int>·{·1,·2,·3,·4,·5·};
  ············var·oddNumbers·=·numbers.Where(n => n % 2 != 0).ToList();
  ········}
  ····}
```

Figure 2-3. *GitHub Copilot offering autocompletions as you type*

Context-Aware Suggestions

Based on the code you are working on, GitHub Copilot can provide context-aware hints. For example, if you are working on collections, it can suggest methods for calculating the average as shown in Figure 2-4.

```
            0 references
✓ ········static·void·Main(string[]·args)
  ········{
  ············var·Scores·=·new·List<int>·{·90,·80,·50,·70,·60·};
  ············var·averageScores·=·Scores.Average();
  ········}
  ····}
```

Figure 2-4. *GitHub Copilot offering context-based code suggestions*

POINT TO NOTE

If you observe in Figure 2-4, we didn't specify our intent via comments; however, GitHub Copilot is aware of the context and based on variable name it provided Average () method as a suggestion.

Context-Aware feature will be super useful when working on a larger code base where Copilot is offering you code suggestions based on the context.

Let's look at this in action in Demonstration 2.

Demonstration 2

Consider you are working on data access layer and have defined a **Product** class; Copilot understands this context. When you start writing methods to retrieve products, it might suggest either database operations or LINQ queries relevant to **Product** objects.

```
public class Product
{
    public int Id { get; set; }
    public string Name { get; set; }
    public decimal Price { get; set; }
}

public class ProductRepository
{
    private List<Product> _products = new List<Product>
{
    new Product { Id = 1, Name = "Laptop", Price = 1200.00m },
    new Product { Id = 2, Name = "Mouse", Price = 25.00m },
    new Product { Id = 3, Name = "Keyboard", Price = 75.00m }
};

    // Method to get all products
```

GitHub Copilot provides suggestions to add GetAllProducts() method name along with the body as shown in Figure 2-5.

```
        5 references
    public class Product
    {
            3 references
            public int Id { get; set; }
            3 references
            public string Name { get; set; }
            3 references
            public decimal Price { get; set; }
    }

        0 references
    public class ProductRepository
    {
            private List<Product> _products = new List<Product>
    {
            new Product { Id = 1, Name = "Laptop", Price = 1200.00m },
            new Product { Id = 2, Name = "Mouse", Price = 25.00m },
            new Product { Id = 3, Name = "Keyboard", Price = 75.00m }
    };

            // Method to get all products
            public List<Product> GetAllProducts()
            {
                return _products;
            }

    }
```

Figure 2-5. *Copilot suggesting GetAllProducts method based on the context*

Accepting and Iterating on Suggestions

Copilot often provides you with multiple suggestions. Pressing Tab is the primary
way to accept any suggestion. Once you accept the GetAllProducts() method, Copilot
immediately suggests the comment "// Method to get a product by ID" before suggesting
the entire method as shown in Figure 2-6. Once you accept the comment, Copilot will
then provide suggestions to next method which is "GetProductById". Copilot provides
methods with proper names, which helps end users to understand the intent just by
reading their names.

```
    // Method to get all products
    0 references
    public List<Product> GetAllProducts()
    {
        return _products;
    }
    // Method to get a product by ID
```

Figure 2-6. *Copilot Iterating on Suggestions providing the next set of comments*

It's important to note that Copilot is an assistant not a replacement. Always review the suggestions for correctness and efficiency and make sure it follows your project's coding standards. Copilot sometimes hallucinates where the suggestion might seem syntactically correct but not logically fit for your needs. The iterative process of accepting, modifying, or rejecting suggestions is key to effective copilot usage. Refer to Figure 2-7, where GitHub Copilot suggests all the methods inside ProductRepository class.

```csharp
0 references
public class ProductRepository
{
    private List<Product> _products = new List<Product>
    {
        new Product { Id = 1, Name = "Laptop", Price = 1200.00m },
        new Product { Id = 2, Name = "Mouse", Price = 25.00m },
        new Product { Id = 3, Name = "Keyboard", Price = 75.00m }
    };

    // Method to get all products
    0 references
    public List<Product> GetAllProducts()
    {
        return _products;
    }
    // Method to get a product by ID
    0 references
    public Product GetProductById(int id)
    {
        return _products.FirstOrDefault(p => p.Id == id);
    }
    // Method to add a new product
    0 references
    public void AddProduct(Product product)
    {
        _products.Add(product);
    }
```

Figure 2-7. *Copilot suggesting all the methods inside ProductRepository class*

Crafting Effective Prompts for GitHub Copilot

Even though GitHub Copilot excels at anticipating and providing meaningful suggestions, its true power is unleashed when you guide it with clear and effective prompts. What do you mean by prompts? In simple terms, a prompt is natural language text describing the task that an AI should perform. There is a whole new concept of Prompt Engineering, which is to enable LLMs to understand and interpret human language.

POINT TO NOTE

From Wikipedia, Prompt Engineering is the process of structuring or crafting an instruction in order to produce better outputs from a Generative Artificial Intelligence (AI) model.

Think of prompting as a way of communicating your intent to an intelligent assistant. The better you articulate your needs through prompts, the better and more useful Copilot's suggestions will be. You can provide prompts to GitHub copilot in various forms including comments, method signatures, or even providing partial code.

Prompts via Comments

Comments are one of the most straightforward ways to provide prompt to GitHub Copilot. You can ask for suggestions by providing your intent in natural language text. The more descriptive and detailed your comments are, the better code suggestions Copilot will give you.

Demonstration 3

In the below code, you would like to implement Factorial method. You provide your intent with a detailed comment (prompt).

```
// This method calculates the factorial of a given non-negative integer.
// It should handle edge cases like 0 and negative numbers
public int CalculateFactorial (int n)
{
}
```

When you place your cursor inside the **CalculateFactorial** method and press Enter, GitHub Copilot will suggest a complete implementation including the logic to handle base cases as shown in Figure 2-8. The comment guided Copilot to not only calculate the factorial but also to consider edge cases while implementing the logic.

```
0 references
public class Test
{
    // This method calculates the factorial of a given non-negative integer.
    // It should handle edge cases like 0 and negative numbers.
    0 references
    public int CalculateFactorial(int n)
    {
        if (n < 0)
        {
            throw new ArgumentException("Input must be a non-negative integer.");
        }
        if (n == 0 || n == 1)
        {
            return 1;
        }
        int result = 1;
        for (int i = 2; i <= n; i++)
        {
            result *= i;
        }
        return result;
    }
}
```

Figure 2-8. *GitHub Copilot offering code suggestions based on prompts provided via comments*

Leveraging Method Signatures and Method Names

Method signatures and method names are implicit prompts which are quite powerful. GitHub Copilot analyzes your method names, its parameters, and the return type to offer relevant code suggestions. A well-defined method is often enough for Copilot to generate its implementation.

Demonstration 4

In the below code, you would like to implement **SortProductsByPrice** method. Please note that we didn't provide any comment or prompt for Copilot, yet it provided full implementation of the method as shown in Figure 2-9.

```
public class Product
{
    public int Id { get; set; }
    public string Name { get; set; }
    public decimal Price { get; set; }
```

```
public List<Product> SortProductsByPrice(List<Product> products)
 {

 }
}
```

```
2 references
public class Product
{
    0 references
    public int Id { get; set; }
    0 references
    public string Name { get; set; }
    0 references
    public decimal Price { get; set; }

    0 references
    public List<Product> SortProductsByPrice(List<Product> products)
    {
        return products.OrderBy(p => p.Price).ToList();
    }
}
```

Figure 2-9. *GitHub Copilot suggesting implementation based on method signature*

Leveraging Partial Code As Prompts

Providing partial code snippet can also serve as an excellent prompt for Copilot. This is extremely helpful when you have certain patterns to follow, and with partial code as prompt, you are triggering Copilot to extend your pattern to complete the implementation details.

Demonstration 5

In the below code, you would like to implement **GetDayOfWeek** method by using switch case statements.

```
public string GetDayOfWeek(int dayNumber)
{
    switch (dayNumber)
```

```
{
    case 1:
        return "Monday";
    case 2:
        // Copilot will likely suggest "Tuesday" and continue for
        other days
```

By providing **Switch Case** statement for one day as partial code (Prompt), GitHub Copilot can analyze the user's intent to use **Switch** statement. So, it will go ahead and offer suggestions to complete the rest of the **Case** statements for the remaining days of the week as shown in Figure 2-10.

```
0 references
public class Week
{
    0 references
    public string GetDayOfWeek(int dayNumber)
    {
        switch (dayNumber)
        {
            case 1:
                return "Monday";
            case 2:
                return "Tuesday";
            case 3:
                return "Wednesday";
            case 4:
                return "Thursday";
            case 5:
                return "Friday";
            case 6:
                return "Saturday";
            case 7:
                return "Sunday";
            default:
                return "Invalid day";
        }
    }
}
```

Figure 2-10. *GitHub Copilot suggesting implementation based on partial code*

Generating Code Documentation

As developers, we are required to maintain comprehensive documentation which is crucial for code maintenance and for team collaboration. GitHub Copilot can automate this process by generating XML documentation for your code written in any language. This significantly saves time and ensures consistency in documentation across all the files in your solution.

To Leverage this feature, simply place cursor on the class or method or property and type "///" as shown in below code.

Demonstration 6

In the code below, we would like GitHub Copilot to generate XML documentation with pre-filled details for the method GetDayOfWeek.

```
///
public string GetDayOfWeek(int dayNumber)
{
    switch (dayNumber)
    {
        case 1:
            return "Monday";
        case 2:
            return "Tuesday";
......
```

Without GitHub Copilot, Visual Studio will only provide you with the basic template when you type "///" as shown in Figure 2-11.

```
        0 references
  ∨  ····public·class·Week
     ····{
  ∨  ·········///·<summary>
     ·········///··
     ·········///·</summary>
     ·········///·<param·name="dayNumber"></param>
     ·········///·<returns></returns>
        0 references
  ∨  ·········public·string·GetDayOfWeek(int·dayNumber)
     ·········{
  ∨  ············switch·(dayNumber)
     ············{
```

Figure 2-11. *Without GitHub Copilot, Visual Studio IDE provides default summary documentation without pre-filled details*

With GitHub Copilot, it will automatically generate XML documentation including pre-filled details about summary, parameter description, and return values based on the code as shown in Figure 2-12.

```
        0 references
  ∨  ···public·class·Week
     ···{
  ∨  ·········///·[▓▓ accept]
     ·········///·Returns the name of the day of the week corresponding to the specified day number.
     ·········///·</summary>
     ·········///·<param·name="dayNumber">An integer representing the day of the week, where 1 corres
     ·········///·<returns>A string representing the name of the day of the week.  Returns "Monday" f
         ///  valid" for any other value.</returns>
        0 references
  ∨  ·········public·string·GetDayOfWeek(int·dayNumber)
     ·········{
  ∨  ············switch·(dayNumber)
     ············{
  ∨  ···············case·1:
     ···················return·"Monday";
```

Figure 2-12. *GitHub Copilot pre-fills details in the XML documentation*

Ask GitHub Copilot

In the next chapter, we will discuss more about GitHub Copilot Chat and its uses, where we can have conversations with the Copilot to get tailored responses for your needs. However, whether you are reviewing your own code before committing or reviewing your teammates' changes in a Pull request or want quick explanation or even quick help, "Ask Copilot" can be an invaluable tool. You can select the code and ask for full explanation or ask to refactor it or even ask to find any bugs in the current implementation.

To open the "Ask Copilot" option, right-click on any file in Visual studio to open context menu. On top, you will see an option "Ask Copilot" as shown in Figure 2-13.

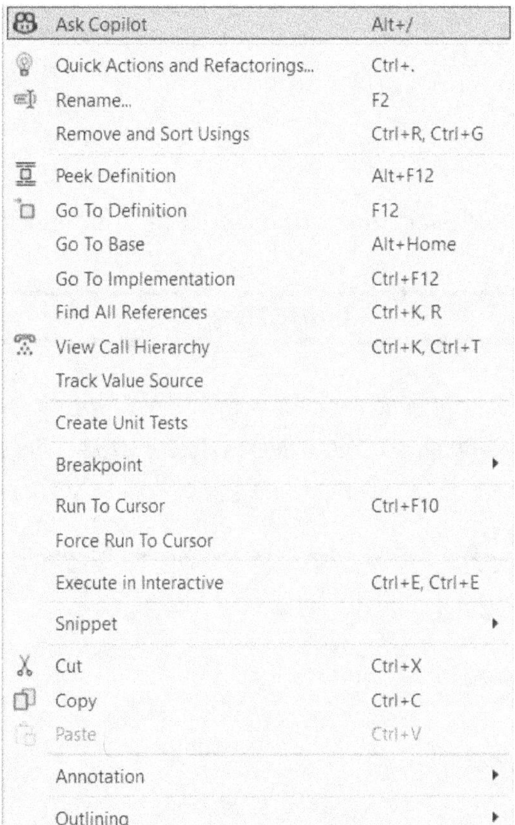

Figure 2-13. *Ask Copilot option on the context menu*

Click on it to open a text box as shown in Figure 2-14, where you update the model based on your requirements and have quick conversations with LLM instead of opening GitHub Copilot Chat window.

Figure 2-14. *Ask Copilot user interface along with model selection*

POINT TO NOTE

---

*When you hover on the Submit button, it clearly says **"Send Prompt to Copilot, and note that responses may be inaccurate"** as shown in Figure 2-15. As the end user, it's your responsibility to always double-check the responses returned from Copilot before using them in your production code.*

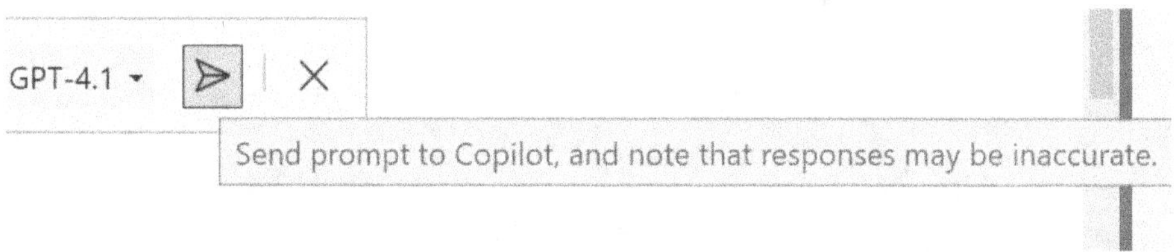

Figure 2-15. *Submit button to send a prompt with a disclaimer*

In the textbox, type "/" (slash) where you will see a virtual drop-down list of built-in slash commands to define your intent as shown in Figure 2-16.

doc	Add documentation comment for this symbol
exp	Start experimental conversation thread
explain	Explain the code
fix	Propose a fix for problems in the selected code
generate	Generate code to answer this question
help	Get help on Copilot chat
optimize	Analyze and improve running time of the selecte...
tests	Create unit tests for the selected code

Figure 2-16. *Out of the box built-in slash commands*

These built in commands are shortcuts to perform common tasks to streamline your workflow.

- **/doc**: Adds documentation comments (like XML comments in C#) for the selected code including class, method, or a property.

- **/exp**: This will start a new "experiment" or "explanation" mode conversation thread where the user is signaling to Copilot that the subsequent input will be a request for an explanation of a code, a concept, or a process.

- **/explain**: Generates detailed explanation of how the selected code works.

- **/fix**: Copilot will propose a solution or suggestion to fix problems in the selected code

- **/generate**: Generates new code snippets or entire methods based on a given prompt or query.

- **/help**: Gets help on Copilot chat.

- **/optimize**: Copilot analyzes the selected code for performance bottlenecks and suggests improvements if any.

- **/tests**: Creates unit tests for the selected code to ensure proper test coverage.

These commands are self-explanatory, and I highly encourage to try all the built-in slash commands on your code base. We will discuss code refactoring, create unit tests, and optimize performance bottlenecks in your code base using **GitHub Copilot Chat** user interface in Chapter 3.

Q&A Session

Q2.1 What is the primary way to accept an inline code suggestion from GitHub Copilot in Visual Studio IDE?

The primary way to accept an inline code suggestion is by pressing the "Tab" key. This will insert the suggested code directly into your editor.

Q2.2 How to ignore an inline code suggestion from GitHub Copilot in Visual Studio IDE?

You can press "Esc" key to ignore and close the code suggestion or simply start typing your own code.

Q2.3 What are the three effective ways to prompt GitHub Copilot to generate code?

The three effective ways to prompt GitHub Copilot are

a. **Writing clear and descriptive comments** that explain your intent in natural language text.

b. **Using well-defined method signatures and method names,** which gives copilot strong hints about the intent.

c. **Providing partial code snippets** to establish what pattern that Copilot should extend on top of your code.

Q2.4 How can GitHub Copilot assist with code documentation in C#?

GitHub Copilot can suggest code documentation for any language, specifically for C#; by typing "///" you can trigger Copilot to automatically generate XML documentation often pre-filling summary, parameter description, and return values based on Method signature.

Q2.5 What is the key difference between using "Ask Copilot" context menu and "GitHub Copilot Chat" window?

The primary difference lies in how they handle context and conversation history.

- **"Ask Copilot"** context menu is designed for quick, focused questions about a specific code snippet. It provides Copilot with precise and isolated context, and the conversation is not persistent (does not store it).

- **"GitHub Copilot Chat"** Window on the other hand is built for conversations, where Copilot remembers the entire history of prompts; this allows Copilot to refine responses based on user inputs without repeating the same code suggestions. The conversation history is also saved in your workspace for future use.

Summary

In this chapter, we explored the core features of using GitHub Copilot within the Visual Studio IDE. We learned how to interact with inline code suggestions, how to accept or ignore them by pressing "Tab" or "Esc" key or typing directly over suggestions. We also discussed effective prompting techniques, like writing clear comments, providing detailed method signatures, or providing partial code as context, which can help Copilot generate more accurate and meaningful suggestions. We also examined how Copilot helps in generating code documentation in C# by typing "///" to trigger suggestions. Overall, this chapter highlighted with better prompts how we can leverage GitHub Copilot to write efficient code along with documentation.

In the next chapter, we will explore how GitHub Copilot integrates into developer workflow across Software development life cycle (SDLC). We will dive deeper into GitHub Copilot Chat user interface, which will help in leveraging Copilot for writing unit tests, optimizing performance bottlenecks, and performing code refactoring. Stay tuned!

CHAPTER 3

GitHub Copilot Chat in Developer Workflow

In Chapter 2, we explored the core features of GitHub Copilot including inline suggestions, autocompletions, and various prompting techniques. We learned how to get meaningful Copilot suggestions by providing effective prompts using comments, method signatures, or through partial code. In this chapter, we will dive deeper into how GitHub Copilot integrates seamlessly into developer workflow. We will discuss GitHub Copilot Chat and explore its features including Ask mode and Agent mode. We will examine how we can leverage GitHub Copilot Chat in various stages of Software Development Life Cycle (SDLC) ranging from rapid prototyping, feature development, refactoring, testing, and during code reviews. The learning objectives for this chapter include the following:

- Understanding how GitHub Copilot accelerates in prototyping to feature development

- Exploring GitHub Copilot Chat features including Ask mode and Agent mode

- Leveraging Copilot for writing unit tests

- Refactoring legacy codebases with the help of GitHub Copilot powered suggestions

- Enhancing code reviews with intelligent Copilot recommendations

By the end of this chapter, you will have mastered the integration of GitHub Copilot Chat into your daily development workflow, which will help in significantly boosting your productivity across all phases of Software development. Let's embark on this journey!

© Naga Santhosh Reddy Vootukuri 2025
N. S. Reddy Vootukuri, *Vibe Coding with GitHub Copilot*, https://doi.org/10.1007/979-8-8688-2196-7_3

GitHub Copilot Chat: Your AI Programming Companion

So far, we have seen GitHub Copilot's inline suggestions which are powerful for immediate code generation; however, GitHub Copilot Chat provides a more interactive and conversational interface for performing complex tasks. It transforms Copilot from a passive suggestion engine into an active coding assistant with whom you can interact, discuss, query, and collaborate. GitHub Copilot Chat user interface remembers previous interactions and can help solve complex multistep problems.

In this section, we will explore the full capabilities of Copilot Chat focusing on its "Ask" and "Agent" modes and how they can be leveraged for various development scenarios along with examples.

Understanding GitHub Copilot Chat User Interface

GitHub Copilot chat can be accessed through various interfaces depending on your development environment.

In Visual Studio IDE:

1. Inside Visual Studio top menu, navigate to View ➤ GitHub Copilot chat as shown in Figure 3-1.

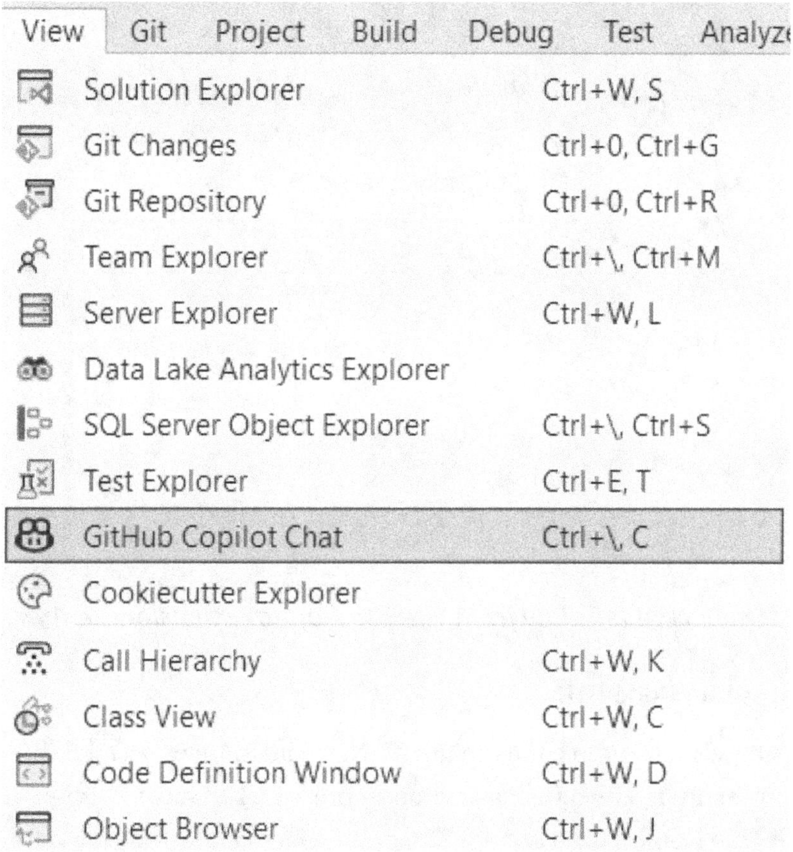

Figure 3-1. Opening GitHub Copilot Chat from view menu

2. You can also access it via the GitHub Icon on the top-right corner, which gets added once you install GitHub Copilot extensions as shown in Figure 3-2.

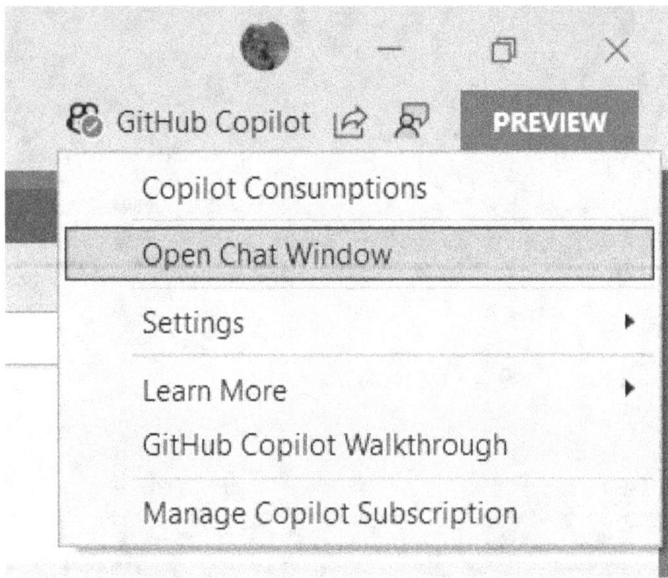

Figure 3-2. *Open chat window from GitHub Copilot extension toolbar*

In Visual Studio Code IDE:

1. Inside Visual studio code top menu, Navigate to View ➤ Open the Command palette or using keyboard, press Ctrl + Shift + P. Type "GitHub Copilot Chat window" to open chat in a new window as shown in Figure 3-3.

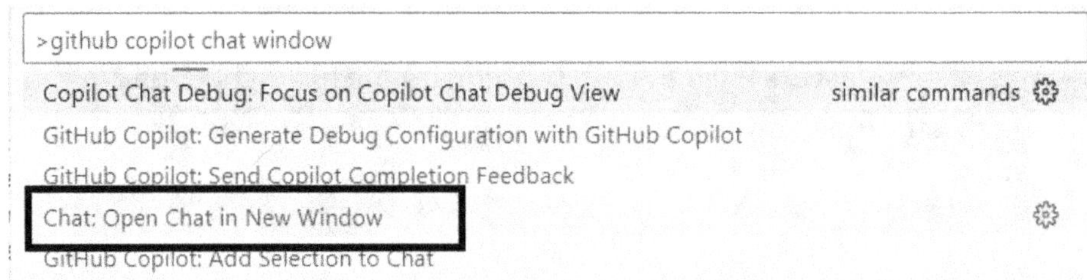

Figure 3-3. *Opening GitHub Copilot Chat window via Command palette*

You can also access Chat window by directly clicking on the GitHub Copilot Icon on the top Activity bar or expand drop-down to select "Open Chat" as shown in Figure 3-4.

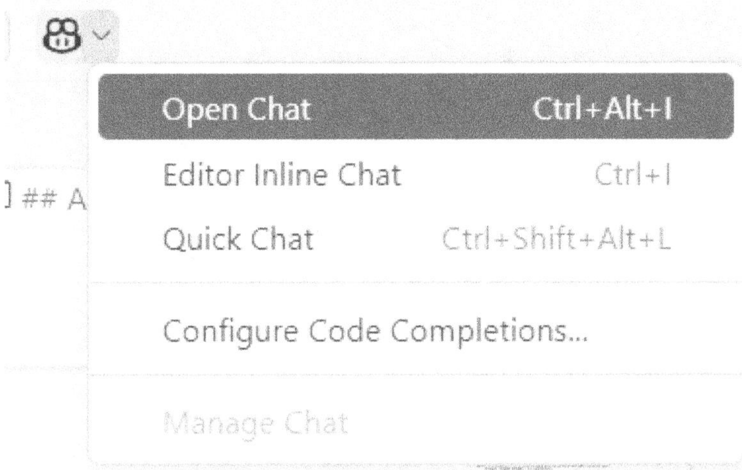

Figure 3-4. Open Chat window via GitHub Copilot Icon on the Activity bar

POINT TO NOTE

In this chapter and throughout the book, we will use Visual Studio 2022 IDE; however, most of the things will work on other IDEs as well, including Visual Studio Code. Wherever needed, I will mention features which are specific to Visual Studio Code.

Once you click on the **"Open Chat Window"** in Visual Studio 2022 IDE, the chat window will dock alongside your other tool windows on the right side, along with Solution Explorer, as shown in Figure 3-5. However, you can drag and adjust to any of the available panes in Visual studio based on your preference.

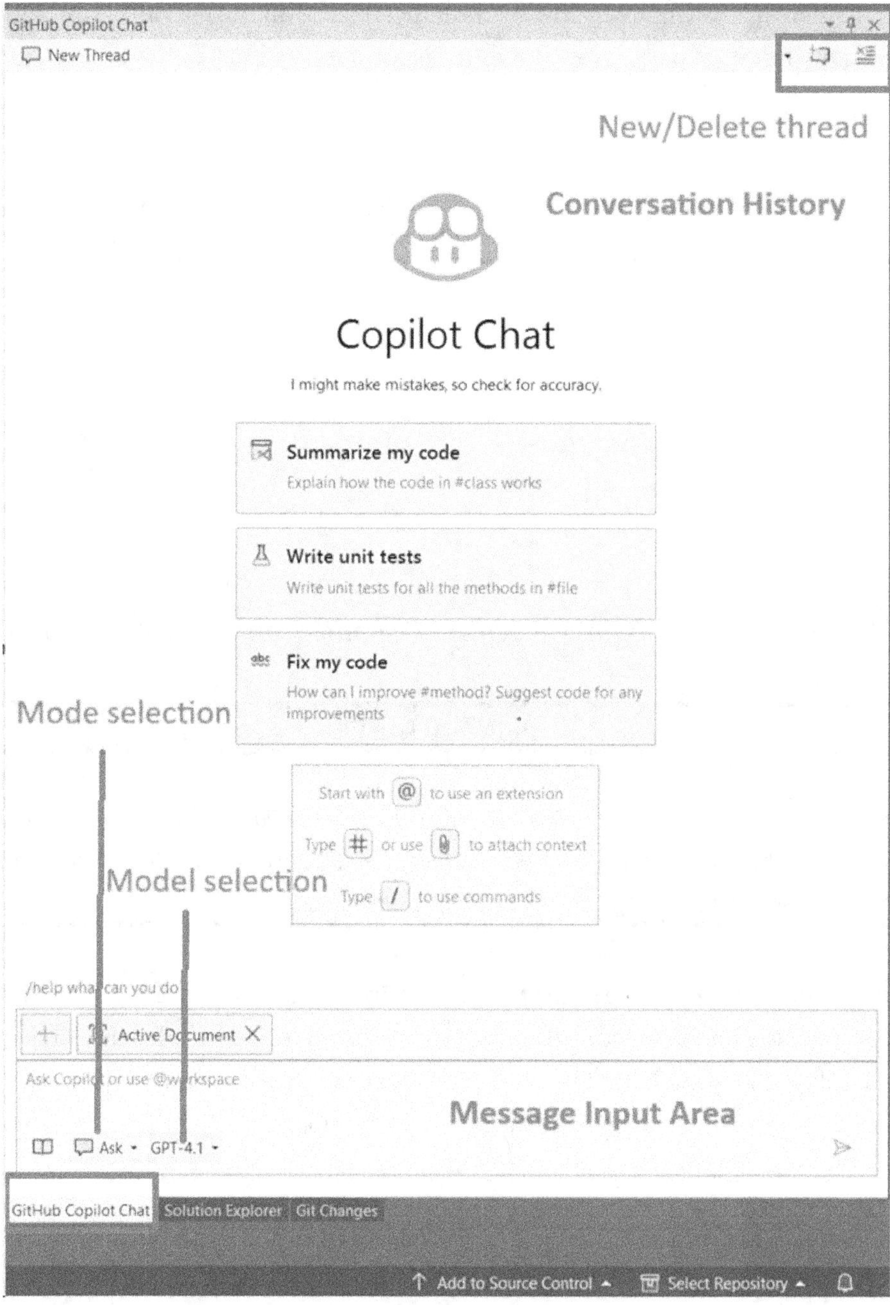

Figure 3-5. *GitHub Copilot Chat window docked next to solution explorer*

The GitHub Copilot Chat user interface consists of several key sections worth mentioning.

a. **Message Input Area:** Bottom text box area where you type your questions and prompt to interact with Copilot.

b. **Conversation History:** Displays ongoing conversations from GitHub Copilot along with previous history.

c. **Show suggested prompts:** Displays out of the box the list of suggested prompts to be selected when interacting with GitHub Copilot as shown in Figure 3-6.

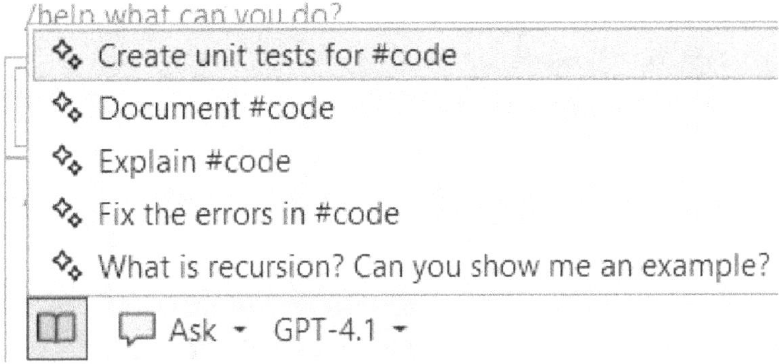

Figure 3-6. *List of suggested prompts to be selected*

d. **Model Selection:** Allows us to choose between different AI models available. At the time of writing this book, ChatGPT-5 (preview) was released and available to use as shown in Figure 3-7.

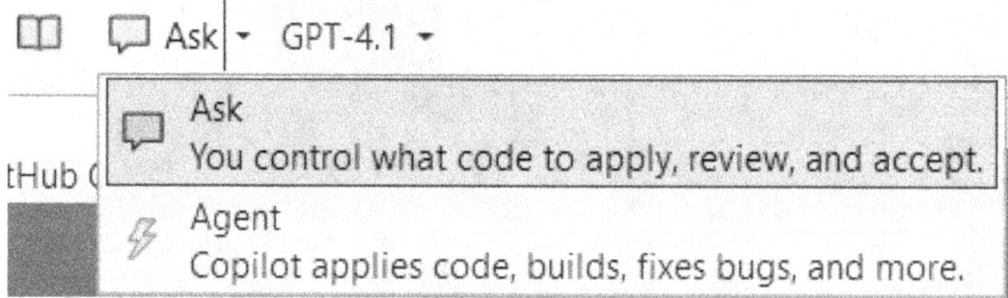

Figure 3-7. *List of available models in GitHub Copilot Chat UI*

    e. **Mode Selection**: Allows us to choose between "Ask" mode and "Agent" mode as shown in Figure 3-8. We will discuss more about these modes in the subsequent sections.

Figure 3-8. *Mode selection in GitHub Copilot Chat UI*

    f. **Create/Delete Thread**: Allows us to create a new thread or delete existing threads to remove history.

POINT TO NOTE

"Thread" refers to ongoing conversation between you and the Copilot within the chat interface. This allows you to ask for code suggestions, code explanations, or even debugging help in an organized manner. By default, conversations (Threads) are saved in the user workspace. If you don't want, you can click on the "Delete Thread" button on the top to remove it from memory.

You can see the list of current and previous threads by clicking on the dropdown next to the "Create new thread" button inside GitHub Copilot Chat window as shown in Figure 3-9.

Figure 3-9. *Displaying the list of all Threads (conversations) within GitHub Copilot Chat window*

Ask Mode vs. Agent Mode in GitHub Copilot Chat

GitHub Copilot Chat offers two distinct interaction modes: **Ask Mode** and **Agent Mode**. Let's understand what these modes and their differences are so that it helps in leveraging Copilot more effectively in various coding scenarios.

Ask Mode is the default conversational mode. In this mode, Copilot acts as a smart assistant that responds to your questions, e.g., code-related queries, and requests for code explanations or generating code snippets. It's like interacting with a knowledgeable peer.

How does it work?

You type a question or request in the message input area (e.g., "How do I write a binary search in C#?"), and Copilot provides a response, often code explanation or a code suggestion.

Scope:

Copilot uses the context of your open files, selection, and recent activity to tailor its responses, but it does not perform actions on your behalf.

Use cases:

- Learning new concepts by interacting with Copilot

- Generating code examples for prototyping

- Debugging help when stuck with failures

- Understanding of new APIs or libraries

Example:

You ask, **"What does the selected method do?"** and Copilot explains the method based on its code and comments as shown in Figure 3-10.

Note   How does Copilot have context about the selected code? Because in the selection area, "Active document" was selected. So, Copilot automatically gets the selected code from the current active document.

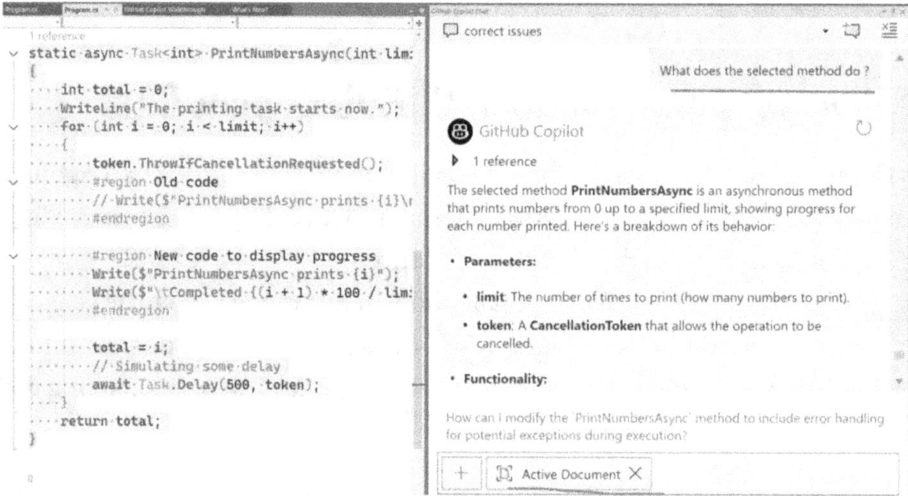

Figure 3-10. *Copilot explaining about selected code from Active document*

While "Ask" mode is excellent for single turn questions and immediate responses, "Agent" mode takes AI assistance to the next level by enabling multistep goal-oriented tasks.

Agent Mode is an action-oriented mode where Copilot acts as an agent that can perform tasks directly in your IDE on behalf of you. These tasks include code refactoring, generating tests, bug fixing, compiling solution, and more. For switching to Agent mode, you need to click the drop-down in the message input area to change to **"Agent Mode"** as shown in Figure 3-11.

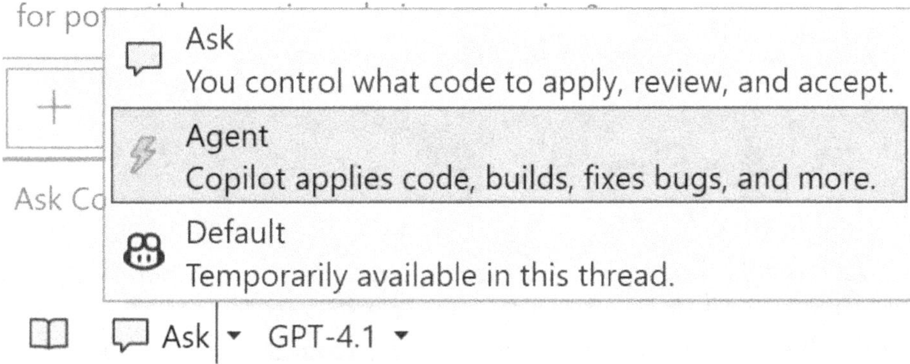

Figure 3-11. *List of various modes available in GitHub Copilot Chat window*

How does it work?

You issue a command by simply typing a prompt (e.g., "Refactor this method to use async/await"), and Copilot not only suggests changes but can also apply them to your codebase and wait for your confirmation to either **"Keep or Undo"** those changes.

Scope:

Copilot can edit files, run tests, compile projects, navigate between code files, and automate repetitive tasks, all within the boundaries of your project and IDE.

Use cases:

- Refactoring code including code optimizations

- Generating boilerplate code

- Executing and fixing tests based on failures

- Applying code suggestions automatically

Example:

Consider typing "Add XML documentation to all public methods in this file", as shown in Figure 3-12.

Figure 3-12. *Agent mode to add XML documentation to all methods in this file*

GitHub Copilot generated response mentioning it found only one public method in this file to add XML documentation, as shown in Figure 3-13.

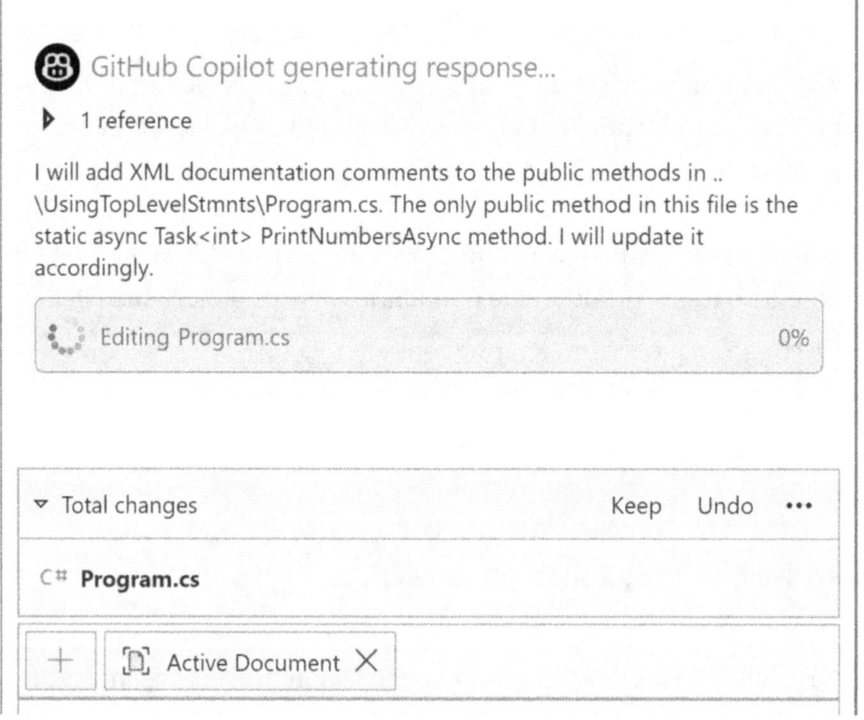

Figure 3-13. *GitHub Copilot generating response to add XML comments*

Copilot generated and inserted the XML comments as shown in Figure 3-14, and now you can either keep or undo the changes. Observe how Copilot not only added XML comments but also prefilled the summary including both return type and method parameter descriptions.

```
+ /// <summary>
+ /// Asynchronously prints numbers up to the specifie
+ /// </summary>
+ /// <param name="limit">The maximum number to print
+ /// <param name="token">A cancellation token to obse
+ /// <returns>The last number printed before completi
  static async Task<int> PrintNumbersAsync(int limit,
  {
      int total = 0;
      WriteLine("The printing task starts now.");
      for (int i = 0; i < limit; i++)
      {
          token.ThrowIfCancellationRequested();
          #region Old code
          // Write($"PrintNumbersAsync prints {i}\n");
          #endregion

          #region New code to display progress
          Write($"PrintNumbersAsync prints {i}");
          Write($"\tCompleted {(i + 1) * 100 / limit}%
          #endregion

          total = i;
          // Simulating some delay
          await Task.Delay(500, token);
      }
      return total;
  }
```

Figure 3-14. *Copilot-generated XML comments including prefilled summary details*

Ask Mode Interactions

Let's look at a few examples in Ask mode on how to effectively communicate with
GitHub Copilot through chat.

Demonstration 1 (Code Explanation)

In this demonstration, we will explore how to use GitHub Copilot to help us with code
explanation and to identify issues within the selected code.

Consider you are working on a complex LINQ query in a codebase as shown in the
code below.

```
// A simple Calculator class with basic arithmetic operations
var result = orders
              . Where(o => o.OrderDate >= DateTime.Now.AddMonths(-3))
              . GroupBy(o => new { o.CustomerId, Month = o.OrderDate.
                Month })
              .Select(g => new
          {

                  CustomerId = g.Key.CustomerId,
                  Month = g.Key.Month,
                  OrderCount = g.Count(),
                  TotalAmount = g.Sum(o => o.TotalAmount),
                  AverageAmount = g.Average(o => o.TotalAmount)
          })
 .OrderBy(x => x.CustomerId) .ThenBy(x => x.Month);
```

You can ask Copilot by typing the below prompt to explain the code and suggest
improvements if any.

Prompt: "Explain what this LINQ query does and suggest any improvements" in the
message input area.

GitHub Copilot returned the response with proper explanation of LINQ query as
shown in Figure 3-15.

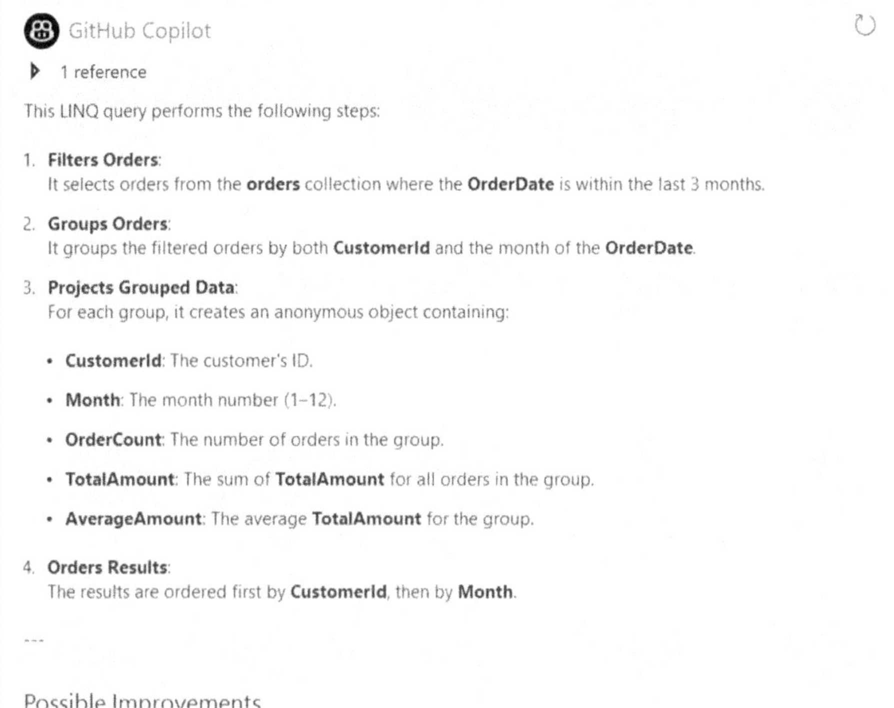

Figure 3-15. *Copilot response explaining LINQ Query*

In the same response generated, Copilot also provided with possible improvements as shown in Figure 3-16.

Possible Improvements:

1. **Date Range Calculation**

    Using **DateTime.Now** in LINQ-to-Entities may not translate well to SQL. If order is an Entity Framework (EF DbSet), consider calculating the date outside the query.

2. **Month Grouping**

    Grouping by **OrderDate.Month** ignores the year. Orders from June 2024 and June 2025 will be grouped together. If you want to separate by year and month, group by both year and month.

Possible Improvements

1. **Date Range Calculation**
   Using **DateTime.Now** in LINQ-to-Entities (e.g., with Entity Framework) may not translate well to SQL. If **orders** is an EF DbSet, consider calculating the date outside the query:

Active Document	Apply

```
var threeMonthsAgo = DateTime.Now.AddMonths(-3);
    var result = orders
        .Where(o => o.OrderDate >= threeMonthsAgo)
        // ... rest of query
```

2. **Month Grouping**
   Grouping by **OrderDate.Month** ignores the year. Orders from June 2024 and June 2025 will be grouped together. If you want to separate by year and month, group by both:

Active Document	Apply

```
.GroupBy(o => new { o.CustomerId, Year = o.OrderDate.Year, Month = o.Ord
    .Select(g => new
    {
        CustomerId = g.Key.CustomerId,
        Year = g.Key.Year,
        Month = g.Key.Month,
        // ...
```

Figure 3-16. *Copilot returning with possible improvements in LINQ query*

In the same chat, when you ask to generate optimized version, it returns the optimized code along with summary of changes as shown in Figure 3-17.

```
var threeMonthsAgo = DateTime.Now.AddMonths(-3);

var result = orders
    .Where(o => o.OrderDate >= threeMonthsAgo)
    .GroupBy(o => new { o.CustomerId, o.OrderDate.Year, o.OrderDate.Mont
    .Select(g => new
    {
        CustomerId = g.Key.CustomerId,
        Year = g.Key.Year,
        Month = g.Key.Month,
        OrderCount = g.Count(),
        TotalAmount = g.Sum(o => o.TotalAmount),
        AverageAmount = g.Average(o => o.TotalAmount)
    })
    .OrderBy(x => x.CustomerId)
    .ThenBy(x => x.Year)
    .ThenBy(x => x.Month);
```

Summary of changes:

- Date range is calculated once, outside the query.

- Grouping now includes year and month, preventing cross-year aggregation.

- Projection uses explicit property names for clarity.
  This version is more robust and maintainable, especially for reporting scenarios.

Figure 3-17. *Copilot-generated optimized code with summary of changes*

Demonstration 2 (Debug Problematic Method)

In this demonstration, let's explore how to leverage "Ask Mode" to help debug a problematic method.

```
// A simple Order Processor class which calculates discounts based on
the orders
public class OrderProcessor
{
    public decimal CalculateDiscount(Order order)
    {
        decimal discount = 0;
        if (order.Items.Count() > 5)
            discount += order.TotalAmount * 0.1m;
        if (order.Customer.IsVip)
            discount += order.TotalAmount * 0.15m;
```

```
    if (order.OrderDate.DayOfWeek == DayOfWeek.Sunday)
        discount += order.TotalAmount * 0.05m;
    return discount;
  }
}
```

There are some significant issues in the above code which include

a. **No maximum discount validation**: Discount on already discounted amount and soon discounts could exceed limits.

b. **Missing null checks**: Could throw exceptions if order or customer is null.

c. **Performance issues**: Using Count () method could be expensive.

d. **Total amount calculation**: If the total amount is not calculated correctly, then the discount will be incorrect.

e. **Discounts could be more**: This is because we are adding discount percentages to the total discount. If all conditions are true, discount could be 30% (0.1+0.15 +0.05), which may not be intended.

Let's ask this question to Copilot and see whether it will identify and fix these issues or not.

Prompt to Copilot Chat: "I'm getting incorrect discount calculations from this method. Can you identify potential issues and suggest fixes?"

Copilot identified several issues and mentioned all of them including the ones we predicted above, as shown in Figure 3-18.

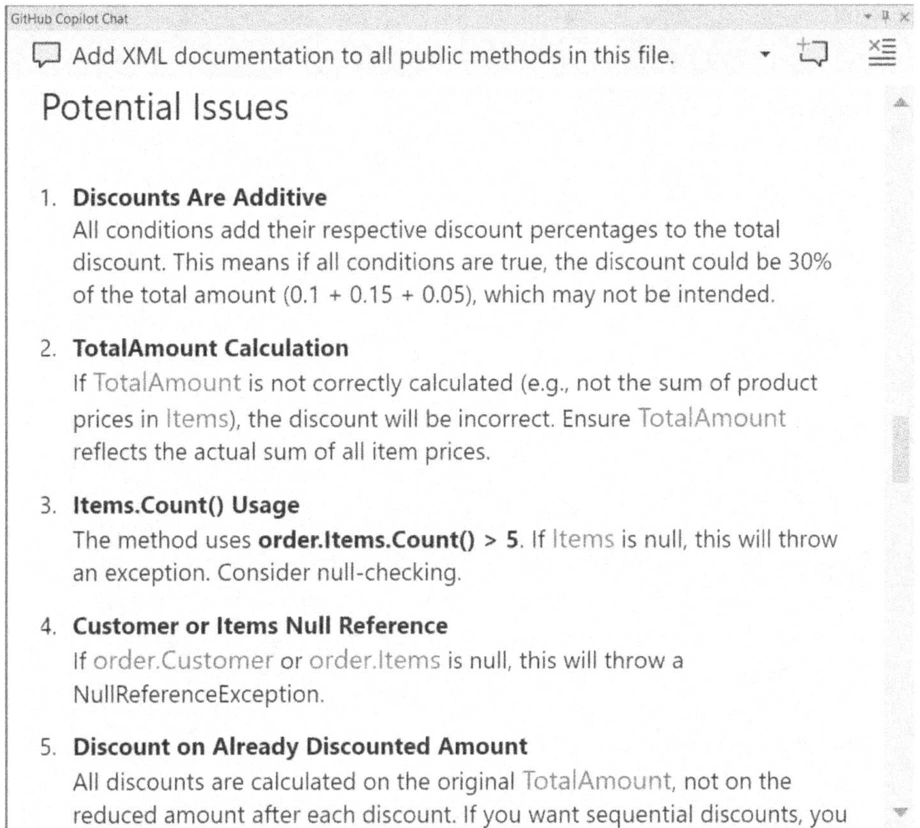

Figure 3-18. *GitHub Copilot's response with identified list of potential issues*

Copilot response also contains "**Suggestions and Fixes**" to the above identified
potential issues as shown in Figure 3-19.

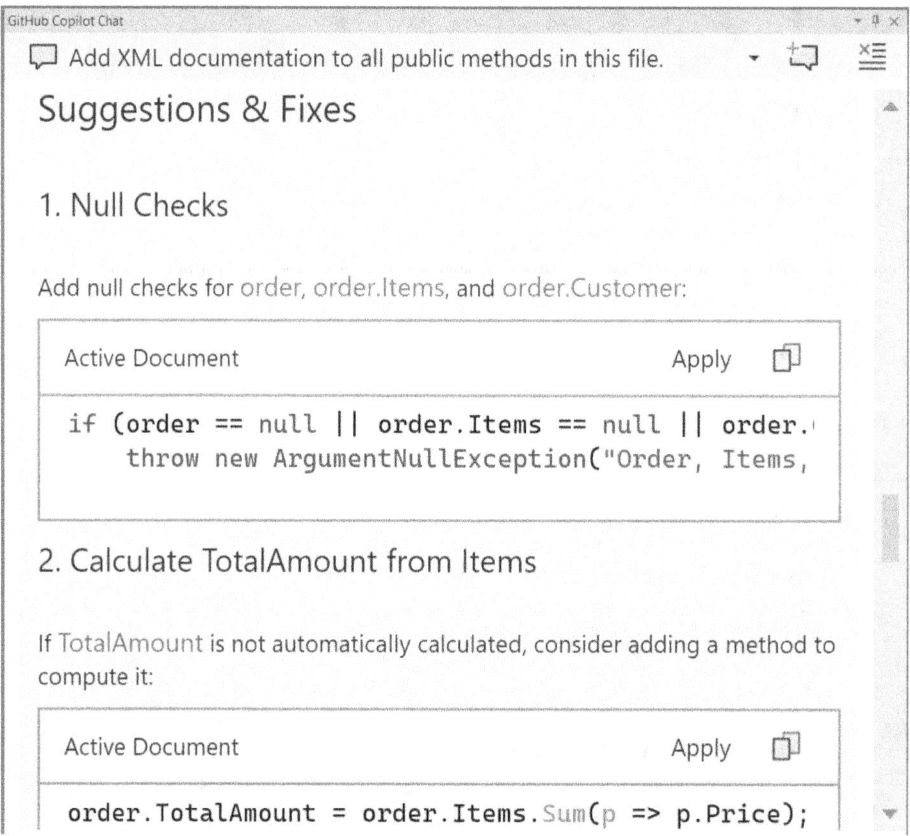

Figure 3-19. *List of suggestions and fixes for the CalculateDiscount() method*

Below is the updated method handling all the issues mentioned above.

```
// A simple Order Processor class which calculates discounts based on
the orders
public class OrderProcessor
{
    public decimal CalculateDiscount(Order order)
    {
    if (order == null || order.Items == null || order.Customer == null)
        throw new ArgumentNullException("Order, Items, or Customer cannot
        be null.");

    decimal baseAmount = order.TotalAmount;
    decimal discount = 0;
```

```
        if (order.Items.Count > 5)
        {
            discount += baseAmount * 0.1m;
            baseAmount -= baseAmount * 0.1m;
        }
        if (order.Customer.IsVip)
        {
            discount += baseAmount * 0.15m;
            baseAmount -= baseAmount * 0.15m;
        }
        if (order.OrderDate.DayOfWeek == DayOfWeek.Sunday)
        {
            discount += baseAmount * 0.05m;
        }
        return discount;
    }
}
```

Quick summary of changes made by Copilot:

    a.   Decide if you want cumulative or sequential discounts.

    b.   Make sure all the referenced properties (like orders and customers) are non-null before checking their values.

    c.   Check if the Total amount is correctly calculated before checking discount logic.

    d.   Document complete discount logic for maintainability and for future use.

Agent Mode Interactions

Agent mode represents hands-free AI-Assisted development. In this mode, you provide Copilot with a high-level objective, and it autonomously plans and executes multiple steps to achieve that goal. Copilot takes complete control over the changes, but it also lets end users to either "Keep or Undo" the changes.

POINT TO NOTE

In traditional Copilot "Ask" mode, you write code or comments, and Copilot suggests completions. In "Agent" mode, you can ask questions, request explanations, or describe tasks and Copilot responds with relevant information. This conversational interface makes complex interactions more intuitive.

Agent Mode can perform various actions but not limited to

    a. Code refactoring

    b. Test generation

    c. Documentation

    d. Bug fixing

    e. Feature implementation

    f. Performance optimization

    g. Interacting with external tools and APIs

For switching to Agent mode, you need to click the drop down in the message input area to change to **"Agent Mode"** as shown in Figure 3-20.

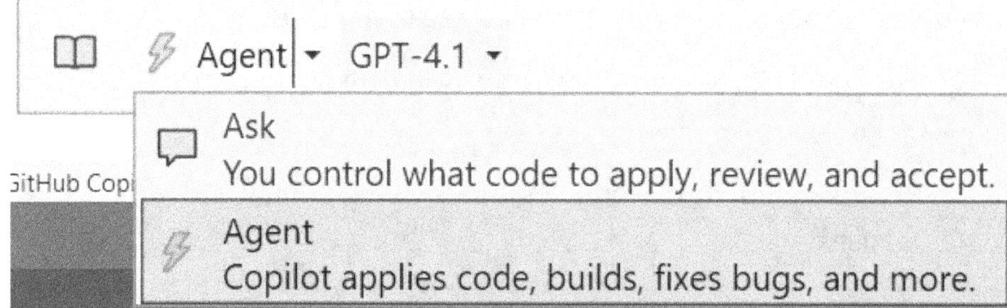

Figure 3-20. *Switching between Ask and Agent modes inside GitHub Copilot Chat*

Let's look at a few examples in Agent mode on how to efficiently leverage Copilot to perform multistep tasks.

Code Refactoring

Code refactoring is considered as a key practice for making sure code is easier to understand and maintainable and can be extended by reducing duplication and clarifying responsibilities. In software engineering, we often write code by following proven design principles like SOLID. However, as soon as code becomes large and systems become complex, we encounter code smells, and refactoring is an important piece to improve structure without changing its behavior, which leads to cleaner, safer, and more testable code.

Demonstration 3

In this demonstration, we will see how Agent mode can refactor a legacy codebase with multiple design issues.

Note   The Order, Customer, and Product classes are omitted to display as the focus is on refactoring **OrderManager** class.

```
// Legacy OrderManager class with multiple issues
public class OrderManager
{
    public List<Order> orders = new List<Order>();
    public string connectionString = "Server=localhost;Database=OrdersDb;Us
    er Id=admin;Password=admin;";

    public void ProcessOrder(int customerId, List<Product> items,
    decimal total)
    {
        // Validate input
        if (customerId <= 0) throw new Exception("Invalid customer");
        if (items == null || items.Count == 0) throw new Exception("No
        items");
        if (total <= 0) throw new Exception("Invalid total");
```

```csharp
// Create order
var order = new Order
{
    Customer = new Customer { Id = customerId },
    Items = items,
    TotalAmount = total,
    OrderDate = DateTime.Now
};
// Save to database
using (var connection = new SqlConnection(connectionString))
{
    connection.Open();
    var command = new SqlCommand($"INSERT INTO Orders (CustomerId,
    Items, TotalAmount, OrderDate) VALUES ({order.Customer.
    Id}, '{string.Join(",", order.Items)}', {order.TotalAmount},
    '{order.OrderDate}')", connection);
    command.ExecuteNonQuery();
}
// Send email
SmtpClient smtp = new SmtpClient("smtp.company.com");
MailMessage mail = new MailMessage();
mail.To.Add("customer@email.com");
mail.Subject = "Order Confirmation";
mail.Body = $"Your order for ${total} has been processed";
smtp.Send(mail);
orders.Add(order);
    }
}
```

We will instruct Copilot Agent mode to refactor the above class by following SOLID design principles and to implement error handling. OrderManager.cs is the only file in our console application apart from program.cs as shown in Figure 3-21. In our prompt to GitHub Copilot, we specify to generate separate files for order, customer, and product classes.

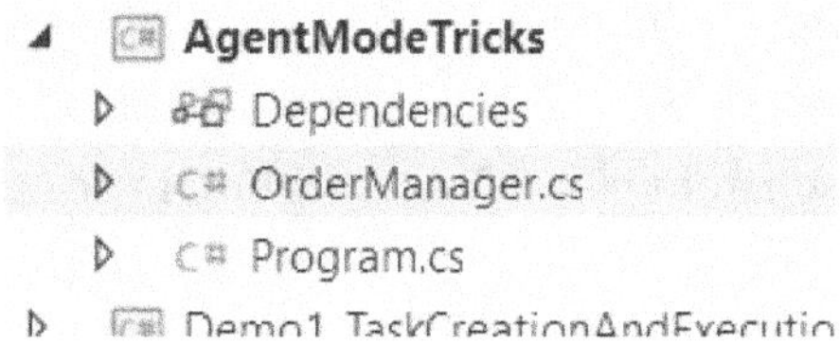

Figure 3-21. *Solution explorer view listing files inside our console application*

Agent Mode Prompt: *"Refactor this OrderManager class following SOLID principles, implement proper error handling, add dependency injection. Also identify and separate classes into separate files."*

GitHub Copilot in Agent mode looked at the entire project and it started working on the tasks. It started working on creating separate files for all the classes by following SOLID principles along with Dependency Injection (DI) as shown in Figure 3-22.

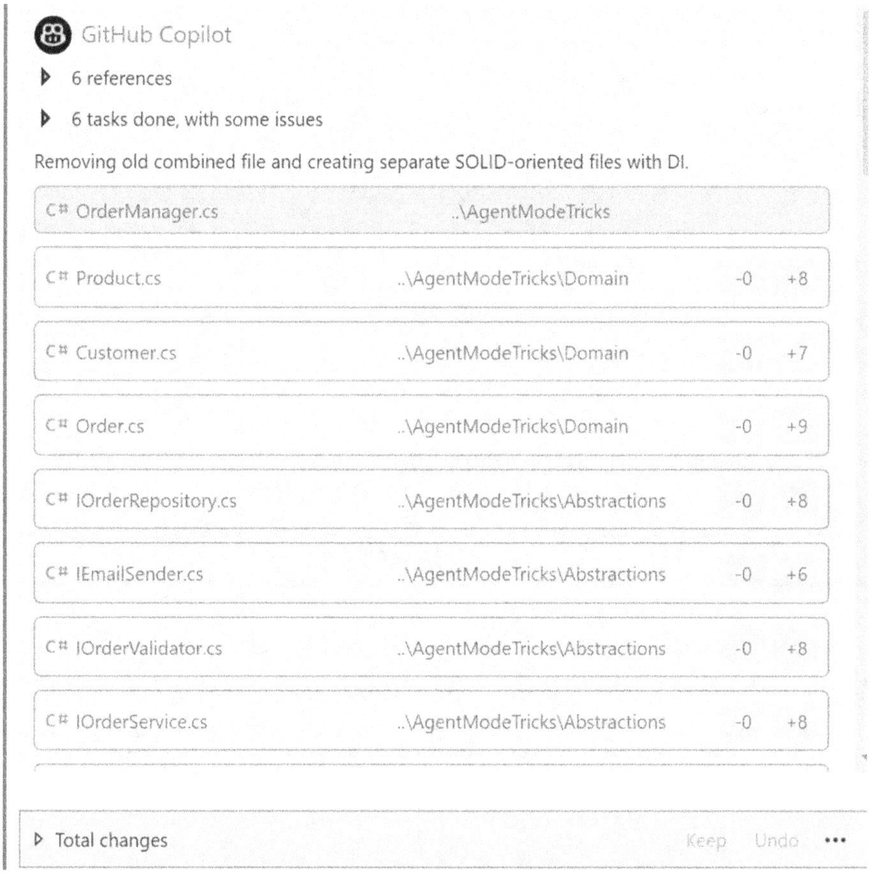

Figure 3-22. *GitHub Copilot generated responses when working in Agent mode*

GitHub Copilot keeps iterating and fixing any errors if there are any compilation issues. Once all the tasks are completed, observe how GitHub Copilot generated multiple folders and files within the current console application by following SOLID principles as shown in Figure 3-23.

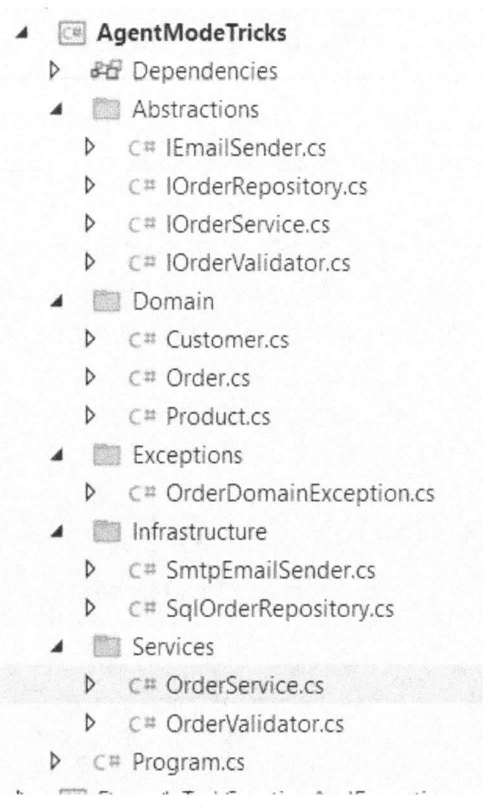

Figure 3-23. List of newly added folders and files by GitHub Copilot

POINT TO NOTE

We didn't mention anything about the folder structure nor file names, yet GitHub Copilot operating in Agent mode is smart enough to understand the intent, breakdown into multiple tasks, iterate on them until it satisfies, and ended up generating all these folders and files.

GitHub Copilot in Agent mode also asks for our permission to run commands in the terminal. Figure 3-24 shows how GitHub Copilot running in Agent mode is waiting for permission from end user. In this case, it wants to add "**Microsoft.Data.SqlClient**" NuGet package.

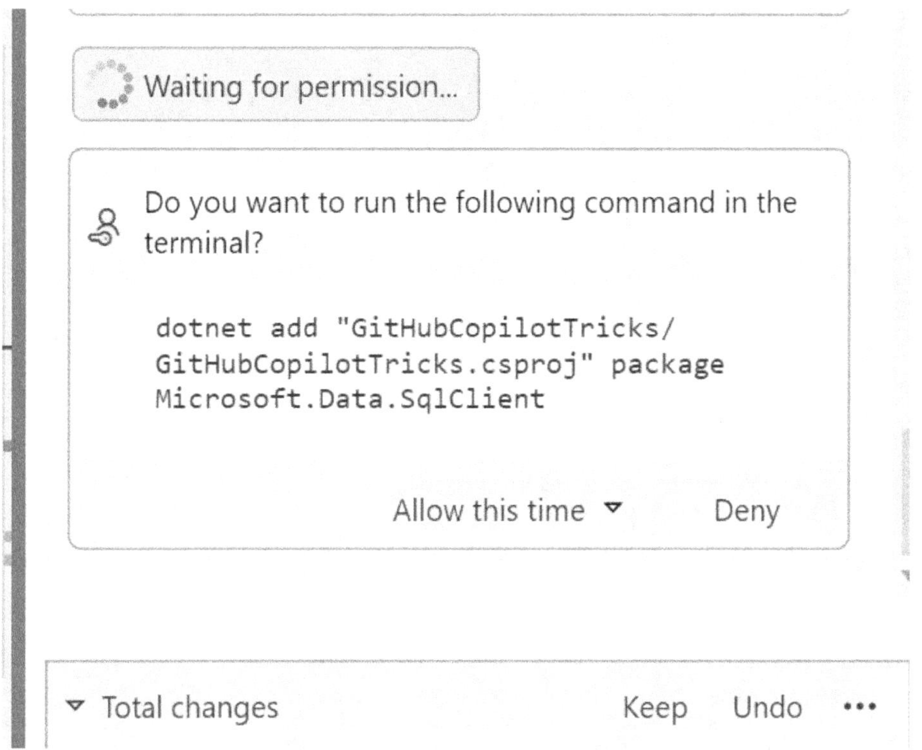

Figure 3-24. *GitHub Copilot is waiting for permission to run commands in terminal*

Once the given task is completed, GitHub Copilot shows a summary of total changes along with an option to **Keep or Undo the changes** as shown in Figure 3-25.

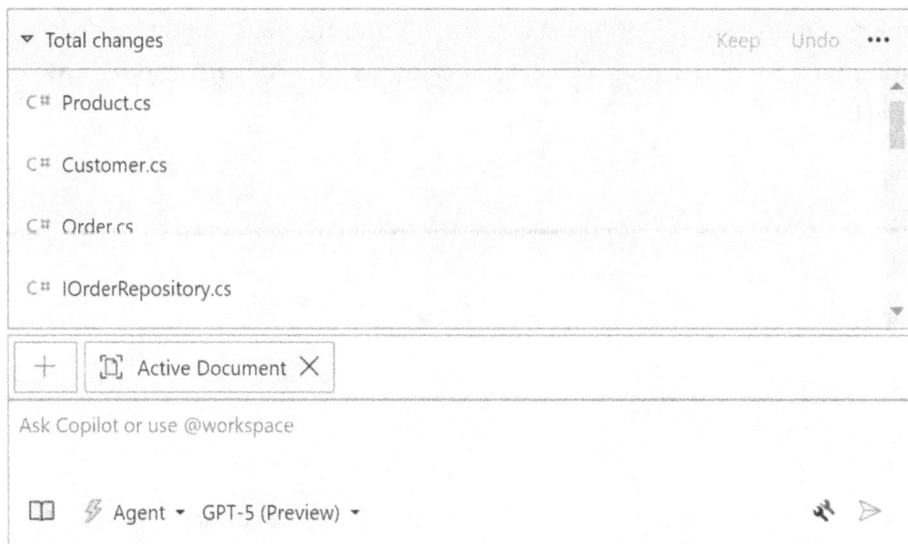

Figure 3-25. *Copilot Agent mode displaying the list of total changes along with the option to keep or discard the changes*

Below is the list of changes performed by GitHub Copilot in Agent mode as shown in Figure 3-26.

a. Split domain models (Order, Product, Customer) into Domain folder.

b. Added abstractions (IOrderService, IOrderRepository, IOrderValidator, IEmailSender).

c. Implemented SqlOrderRepository with parameterized SQL.

d. Implemented SmtpEmailSender.

e. Added OrderValidator and OrderService with error handling.

f. Added domain exception.

g. Introduced dependency injection in Program.cs.

h. Added Microsoft.Extensions.DependencyInjection package.

i. Removed insecure inline SQL and string concatenation email logic.

j. Removed obsolete combined OrderManager file.

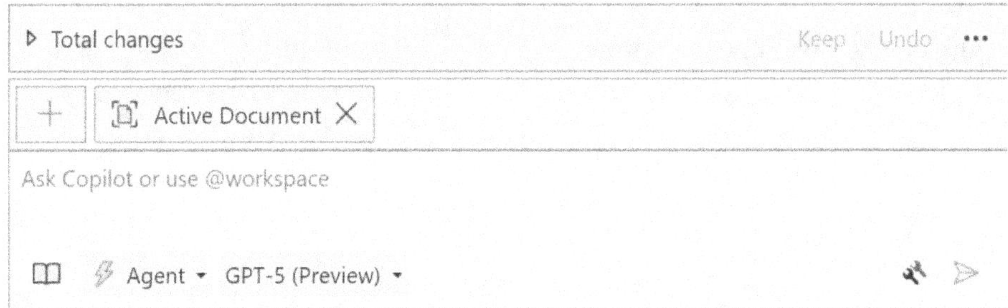

Figure 3-26. *Summary of changes done by GitHub Copilot in Agent mode*

In Summary, Agent mode not only refactored monolithic class but also created production-ready architecture following SOLID principles. It separated out concerns, implemented proper error handling, fixed security issues, and made code testable and maintainable.

Unit Tests Generation

Testing is an important aspect of software development, which ensures code is functional, reliable, and maintainable. However, writing and maintaining comprehensive test suites can be time-consuming. GitHub Copilot has a full understanding of testing patterns/frameworks and excels at generating tests by including supporting edge cases, which developers might have overlooked.

Demonstration 4

We will build on top of the same solution where we left in demonstration 3.

In this demonstration, we will instruct GitHub Copilot in Agent mode to generate Unit tests to make sure code is working as expected. Unit tests are mainly focused on testing individual components and in isolation. Copilot can generate unit tests that cover various scenarios ranging from happy paths to edge cases to error conditions.

Agent Mode Prompt: *"Generate comprehensive unit tests for **Order Service class including ProcessOrderAsync method** using xUnit, use Moq for mocking and create these tests in a separate testing project."*

GitHub Copilot in Agent mode started generating responses and it did ask some clarifying questions before working on the task. Figure 3-27 shows how it has created test projects along with adding NuGet packages for xUnit and Moq. Observe how GitHub Copilot iterated and fixed the build failures as soon as new test projects were created. It made sure to fix the build issue before generating comprehensive test suite.

GitHub Copilot

▶ 3 references

I'll help create comprehensive unit tests for the OrderService using xUnit and Moq. First, let's create a test project and add the necessary packages.

| AgentModeTricks.Tests.csproj | ..\AgentModeTricks.Tests | -0 | +30 |

| OrderServiceTests.cs | ..\AgentModeTricks.Tests\Services | -0 | +149 |

❌ Build failed

| OrderManager.cs | ..\GitHubCopilotTricks | -2 | +6 |

✓ Build successful

I've created a comprehensive test suite for the OrderService with the following test cases:

1. **ProcessOrderAsync_ValidOrder_ShouldSucceed**

   - Tests the happy path where order processing succeeds

   - Verifies order details are correctly set

   - Confirms all dependencies are called once with correct parameters

2. **ProcessOrderAsync_WhenValidationFails_ShouldPropagateException**

Figure 3-27. GitHub Copilot in Agent mode working on generating unit tests

Comprehensive test suite for the OrderService class generated by Copilot:

1. ProcessOrderAsync_ValidOrder_ShouldSucceed

    - Tests the happy path where order processing succeeds

    - Verifies order details are correctly set

    - Confirms all dependencies are called once with correct parameters

2. ProcessOrderAsync_WhenValidationFails_
   ShouldPropagateException

   • Tests validation failure scenario

   • Verifies the domain exception is propagated

   • Ensures repository and email sender are not called

3. ProcessOrderAsync_WhenRepositorySaveFails_
   ShouldWrapException

   • Tests database error handling

   • Verifies exception wrapping

   • Ensures email sender is not called after repository failure

4. ProcessOrderAsync_WhenEmailFails_ShouldWrapException

   • Tests email sending failure

   • Verifies exception wrapping

   • Confirms repository save was still attempted

5. ProcessOrderAsync_WhenInvalidCustomerId_
   ShouldThrowException

   • Theory test for invalid customer IDs (0 and -1)

   • Verifies validation exceptions

   • Tests with multiple data points using [Theory] and [InlineData]

Note   For testing Invalid Customer ID, GitHub Copilot also added a check
for invalid customer IDs (0 and -1). It's a small detail but often overlooked by
developers to check for invalid IDs.

GitHub Copilot returned with a confirmation question: *"Would you like me to add
any additional test scenarios or make any modifications to the existing ones?"* as shown
in Figure 3-28. Once it gets the confirmation, it went ahead and created these tests in the
newly added test project.

All tests follow xUnit best practices and maintain AAA (Arrange-Act-Assert) pattern. The mocks are properly setup to verify both successful calls and error conditions.

Would you like me to add any additional test scenarios or make any modifications to the existing ones?

Was this helpful? 👍 👎

no that would be all

GitHub Copilot

▶ 2 references

Based on the current state and the request, the test coverage looks comprehensive but let's ensure it runs correctly. Let's run the build to verify everything is properly set up:

✓ Build successful

Great! The build is successful. Our test suite for the OrderService now provides comprehensive coverage with:

1. Successful order processing

Figure 3-28. *GitHub Copilot iterating on the tasks and asking questions to include any additional test scenarios*

As usual, once all the tasks are completed, GitHub Copilot displays the list of total changes at the bottom with an option for end user to either **keep or discard (Undo)** as shown in Figure 3-29.

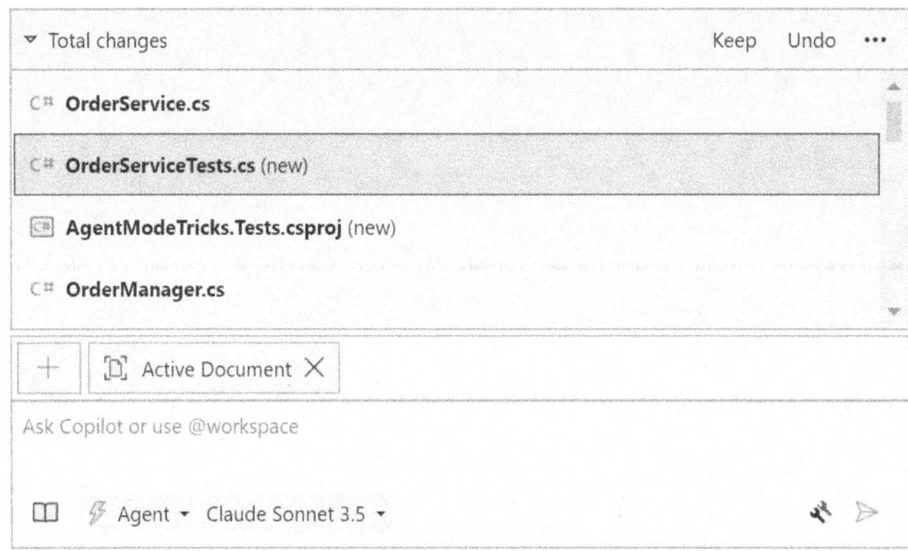

Figure 3-29. *Summary of total changes with an option to Keep or Undo*

We are not displaying full lines of code (tests) generated by copilot; below is just an excerpt from the generated tests file.

```
// Unit tests for OrderManager class testing functionality
public class OrderServiceTests
{
    ..........

    [Theory]
    [InlineData(0)]
    [InlineData(-1)]
public async Task ProcessOrderAsync_WhenInvalidCustomerId_
ShouldThrowException(int customerId)
 {
    // Arrange
    var items = new List<Product> { new() { Name = "Test Product", Price =
    10.0m } };
    var total = 10.0m;
 _validatorMock
    .Setup(x => x.Validate(customerId, items, total))
    .Throws(new OrderDomainException("Invalid customer"));
```

```
// Act & Assert
var exception = await Assert.ThrowsAsync<OrderDomainException>(
    () => _sut.ProcessOrderAsync(customerId, items, total));

Assert.Equal("Invalid customer", exception.Message);
}

    ............

}
```

However, you can see how Copilot generated unit tests based on xUnit framework and used Moq NuGet package for mocking. Figure 3-30 shows an excerpt from OrderServiceTests.cs class containing the unit tests generated by GitHub Copilot.

OrderServiceTests.cs | OrderService.cs | AgentModeTricks.Tests.csproj | OrderDomainException.cs | IOrderValidator.cs | Customer.cs | Order.cs | Product.cs

AgentModeTricks.Tests.Services.OrderServiceTests | ProcessOrderAsync_WhenValidationFails_ShouldPropagateException()

```
public class OrderServiceTests
{
    private readonly Mock<IOrderValidator> _validatorMock;
    private readonly Mock<IOrderRepository> _repositoryMock;
    private readonly Mock<IEmailSender> _emailSenderMock;
    private readonly OrderService _sut;
    private readonly CancellationToken _ct;

    public OrderServiceTests()
    {
        _validatorMock = new Mock<IOrderValidator>();
        _repositoryMock = new Mock<IOrderRepository>();
        _emailSenderMock = new Mock<IEmailSender>();
        _sut = new OrderService(_validatorMock.Object, _repository
        _ct = CancellationToken.None;
    }

    [Fact]
    public async Task ProcessOrderAsync_ValidOrder_ShouldSucceed()
    {
        // Arrange
        var customerId = 1;
        var items = new List<Product> { new() { Name = "Test Produ
        var total = 10.0m;

        Order? savedOrder = null;
        _repositoryMock
            .Setup(x => x.SaveAsync(It.IsAny<Order>(), _ct))
```

issues found | Keep | Undo | Ln: 222 | Ch: 2 | SPC | CRLF

Figure 3-30. *Copilot-generated OrderServiceTests class using xUnit and Moq*

POINT TO NOTE

As with any Copilot-generated responses, it's your responsibility as a consumer to check the functionality, accuracy, and correctness of the code before using it in production.

Not just unit tests generation, you can leverage GitHub Copilot for writing Integration tests as well to cover end to end workflows.

Code Reviews

Code Reviews are an important practice in Software Development life cycle (SDLC) to ensure code is of high quality by adhering to coding standards. It's a final step to identify and catch any bugs before they reach production. Code bugs are inevitable; however, we can fix known issues with code reviews. Usually, Team members or managers are responsible for looking at pull requests to identify any code smells and to provide with meaningful feedback to the author in mitigating those risks.

While GitHub Copilot cannot replace the critical thinking of a human reviewer, it can serve as a valuable assistant in identifying potential issues, recommending improvements, adhering to clean coding standards, and providing intelligent suggestions.

Copilot has awareness of common security vulnerabilities (like SQL injection, Cross-site scripting (XSS), or detecting hardcoding of sensitive information related to credentials) based on its training data. Copilot can play a significant role when it comes to identifying security issues. However, we cannot simply rely only on Copilot review. We should do threat modelling and consult security experts within the team for reviewing.

Note   Authors submitting Pull Requests (PRs) and reviewers examining PRs can leverage Copilot during code review process.

Demonstration 5

For the same code used in Demonstrations 3 and 4, let's ask Copilot to review the code changes and create a comprehensive checklist.

Note   Current code was generated by Copilot if you followed demonstrations 3 and 4.

Agent Mode Prompt: *"Create a comprehensive code review checklist for the OrderManager project that can also cover security and performance related issues."*

GitHub Copilot carefully analyzed code and created a comprehensive code review checklist focusing on security and performance as shown in Figure 3-31.

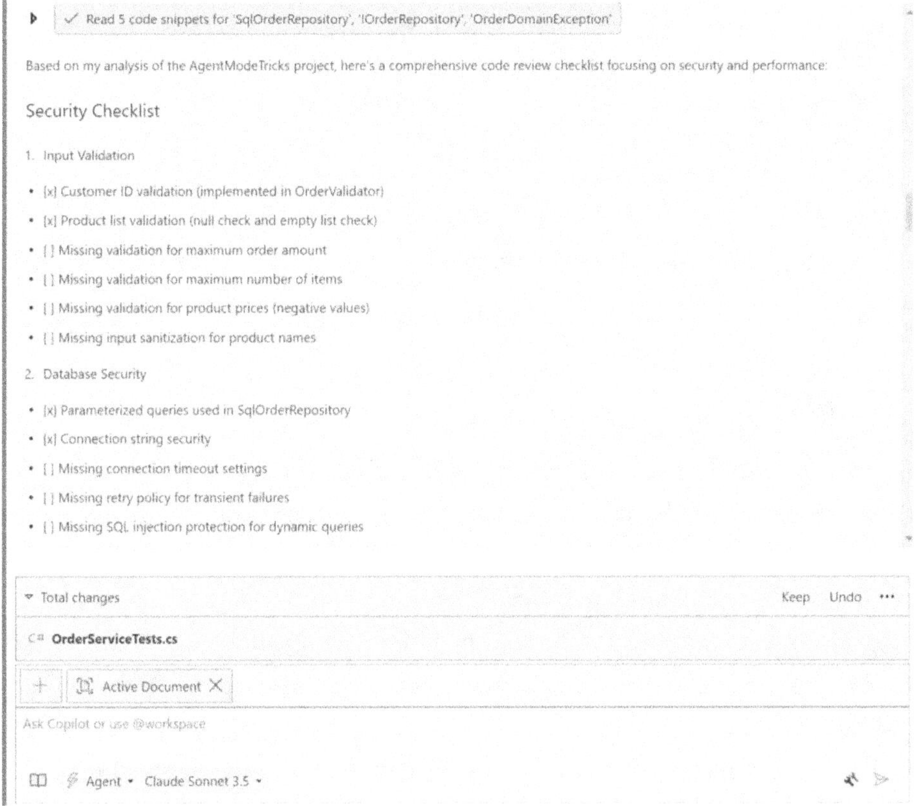

Figure 3-31. Copilot response with a comprehensive list of security checklist

Not just identifying potential issues, GitHub Copilot also suggests recommendations for improvement in the same response as shown in Figure 3-32.

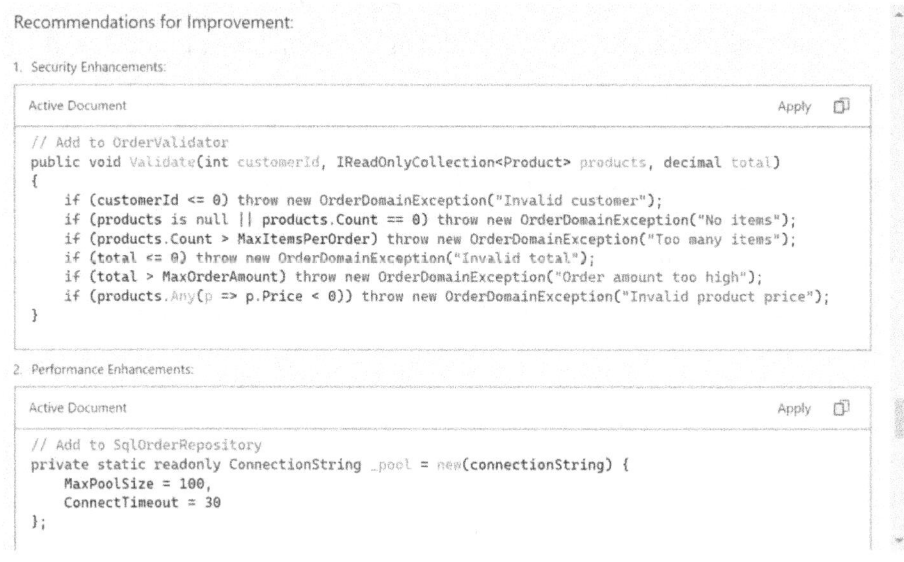

Figure 3-32. *Copilot also returning recommendations for improvement in the same response*

Q&A Session

Q1.1 What does thread mean in GitHub Copilot Chat world?

In the context of GitHub Copilot Chat, a "thread" refers to the ongoing conversation between you and Copilot within the chat interface. Each thread consists of your questions, Copilot's responses, and any follow-up interactions. This allows you to ask for code suggestions, explanations, or debugging help in a continuous, organized manner.

Q1.2 What is the key difference between Ask Mode and Agent Mode in GitHub Copilot Chat?

Ask Mode is a conversational mode where Copilot responds to questions and provides code explanations or suggestions but doesn't perform actions, whereas **Agent Mode** is action-oriented, where Copilot can directly perform multistep tasks like refactoring code, generating tests, or applying changes to your codebase by asking for confirmations.

Q1.3 How can you access GitHub Copilot Chat in Visual Studio Code?

You can access it in two ways:

1. Opening Command Palette (Ctrl+Shift+P) and typing "GitHub Copilot Chat window".

2. Clicking the GitHub Copilot icon on the Activity bar and selecting "Open Chat".

Q1.4 What are the main components of the GitHub Copilot Chat user interface?

The main components include

- Message Input Area (for typing prompts)

- Conversation History (for displaying ongoing conversations)

- Show Suggested Prompts (quick prompt suggestions)

- Model Selection dropdown (for choosing AI models)

- Mode Selection dropdown (for choosing Ask/Agent mode)

- Create/Delete Thread functionality (for creating new threads)

Q1.5 What should you verify when using Copilot-generated code in production?

You should always verify the functionality, accuracy, and correctness of Copilot-generated code. Check for security vulnerabilities, performance implications, and adherence to coding standards, and ensure the code meets your specific requirements before using it in production.

Summary

In this chapter, we explored GitHub Copilot Chat and how it elevates AI assistance from being passive inline suggestions to being an active coding partner via conversational interactions. We examined two distinct interactive modes in GitHub Copilot – Ask mode and Agent mode and their usage with real-world code examples.

Overall, this chapter highlighted how GitHub Copilot Chat fits neatly into the developer workflow of Software development life cycle (SDLC) from rapid prototyping to code reviews.

In the next chapter, we will explore how to interact and leverage GitHub Copilot on the Web.

CHAPTER 4

GitHub Copilot on the Web

In Chapter 3, we introduced GitHub Copilot as a powerful AI pair programmer and explored GitHub Copilot's capabilities in detail within Visual Studio IDE (Integrated development environment). This chapter will focus heavily on leveraging GitHub Copilot's powerful features directly through GitHub.com web interface. We will explore how these features can enhance your development workflow, improve code quality, and streamline collaboration without leaving your web browser. From sending pull requests descriptions to repository analysis to bringing in intelligent code suggestions in the web editor, we will uncover the full potential of GitHub Copilot on the web capabilities.

The learning objectives for this chapter include the following:

- GitHub Copilot web editor integration and code suggestions

- Using GitHub Copilot to manage project work items and tasks

- Leveraging Copilot Chat in performing code repository analysis

- Utilizing Copilot for improving Pull requests by sending automatic description based on the edited changes

- Generating comprehensive documentation and readme files directly on the github.com website

- Mastering Copilot in proving valuable suggestions during code reviews

- Exploring GitHub Spark for quickly developing prototypes

By the end of this chapter, you will become proficient in using GitHub Copilot's web-based features, which will help in improving productivity, collaborating more effectively with your teammates, and maintaining high-quality code bases. The GitHub web interface is no longer just for hosting code, but it has evolved into a comprehensive AI-native development platform.

GitHub Copilot Integration on Web Editor

The GitHub Web Editor powered by Visual Studio Code for the web provides a complete development environment directly in your browser, and it comes with full GitHub Copilot Integration. There are multiple ways you can access this powerful web editor interface.

Using Keyboard Shortcut

While viewing any repository on GitHub.com, simply press the period (.) key to instantly launch the web editor. This is the fastest method and works for almost any repository page, file view, or directory listing.

Figure 4-1 shows how `https://github.com/github/awesome-copilot` repository is opened in the web editor after pressing (.) button.

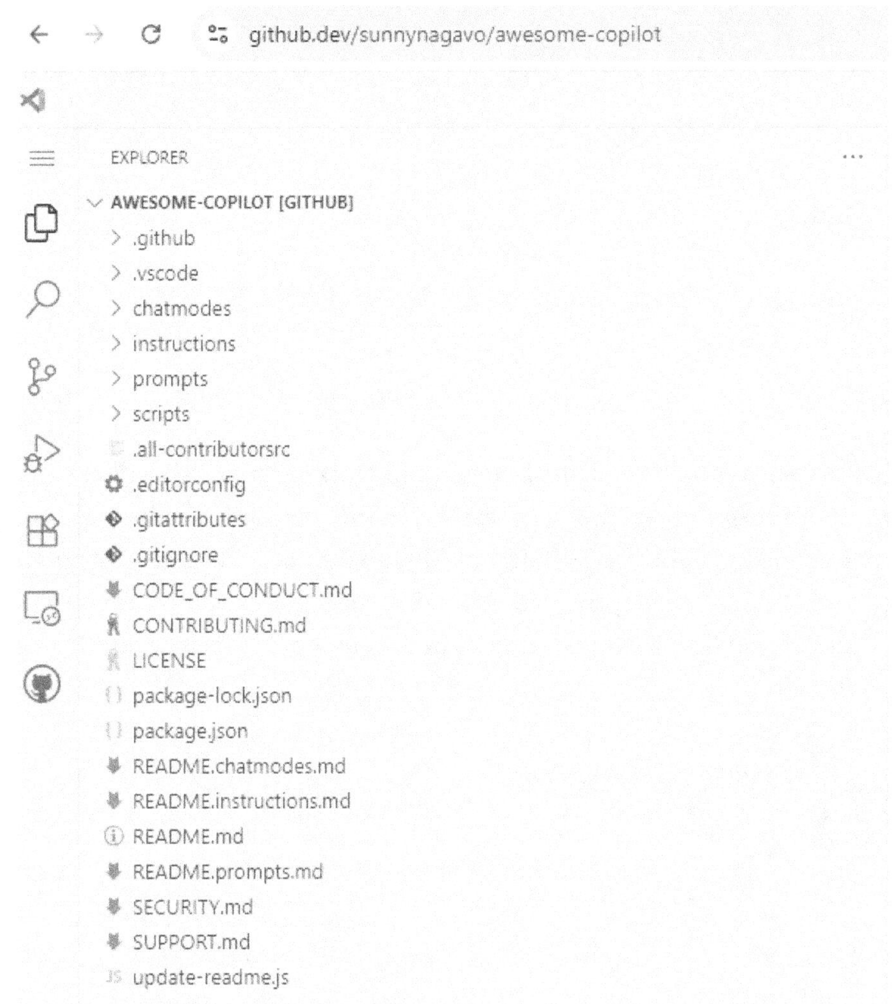

Figure 4-1. *GitHub repository opened in web editor mode*

URL Modification

Transform any GitHub repository URL by changing the domain from github.com to github.dev; it takes a few seconds to set up your web editor, as shown in Figure 4-2, before opening the web editor. For example:

Original: `https://github.com/github/awesome-copilot`

Web Editor: `https://github.dev/github/awesome-copilot`

Figure 4-2. *Displays "Setting up your web editor" message before opening*

Inside the web editor, there is an **"Extensions: Marketplace"** tab where you can install various extensions from marketplace. Type GitHub Copilot in the search to list all the available extensions. You can install the "GitHub Copilot – Your AI pair programmer" extension from GitHub, which provides rich inline coding suggestions as you type; however, "GitHub Copilot Chat" extension is not available on this web editor, as shown in Figure 4-3.

Figure 4-3. *Displays GitHub Copilot Chat extension unavailable in Visual Studio code for the web*

Note   To leverage GitHub Copilot chat on the web editor, GitHub codespaces will come to our rescue.

GitHub Codespaces

Navigate to any repository on Github.com and click on green "code" button, as shown in Figure 4-4.

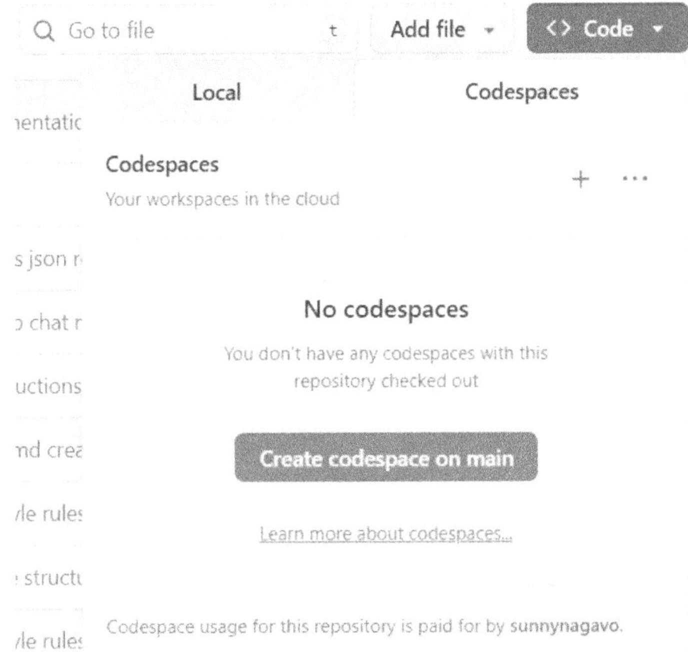

Figure 4-4. Displays green code button to create codespaces

Select the "Codespaces" tab and click on create, which will take a couple of minutes to create and open Codespaces, which is nothing but opening code on web editor. A new web editor is opened on a new tab, and it looks exactly like Visual Studio code, as shown in Figure 4-5.

Note   GitHub copilot icon appears next to the search bar, and you can also open copilot chat window and interact with it on the codespaces.

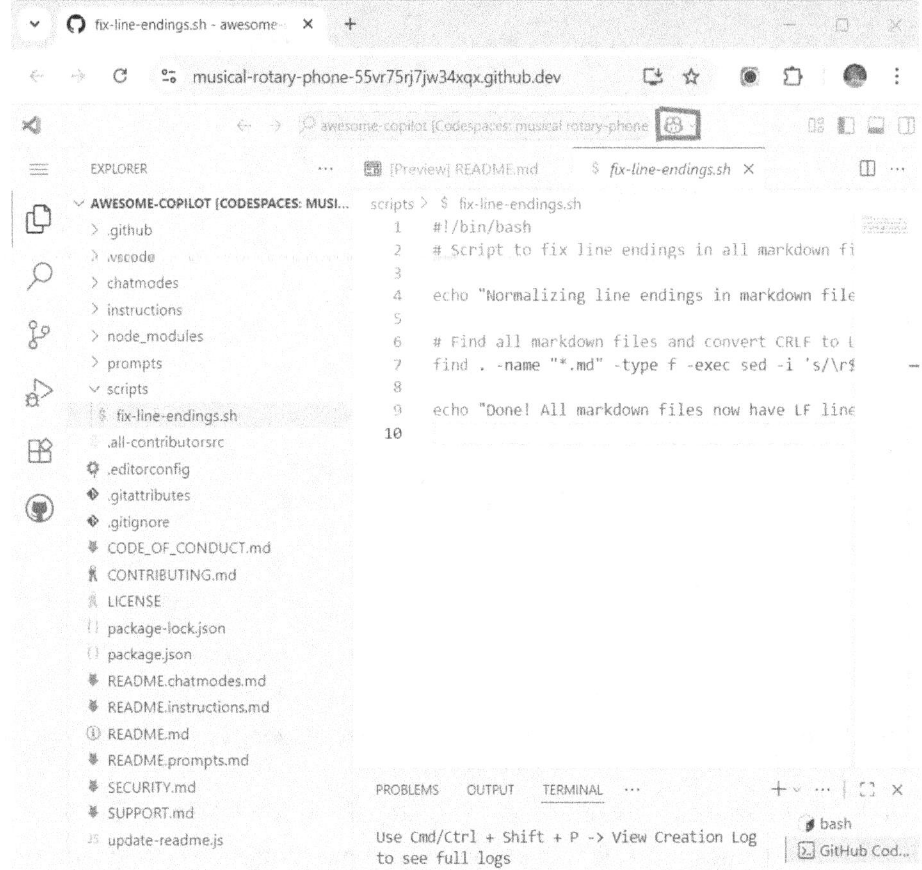

Figure 4-5. *Codespace web editor with GitHub Copilot Icon next to the search bar*

POINT TO NOTE

A Codespace will automatically stop running after a period of inactivity. By default, this period is 30 mins, but users can customize this in their personal settings on GitHub. The timeout only stops but does not delete it and all data is preserved. Codespaces that have been stopped and remained inactive for a specified period will be automatically deleted. The default retention period for automatic deletion is 30 days.

Observe the URL "`https://musical-rotary-phone-55vr75rj7jw34xqx.github. dev/`", which is different as compared to opening web editor using **github.dev,** and these unique names **(musical-rotary-phone)** are created automatically by GitHub Codespaces. Figure 4-6 displays the list of all created codespaces that are still active on the current branch.

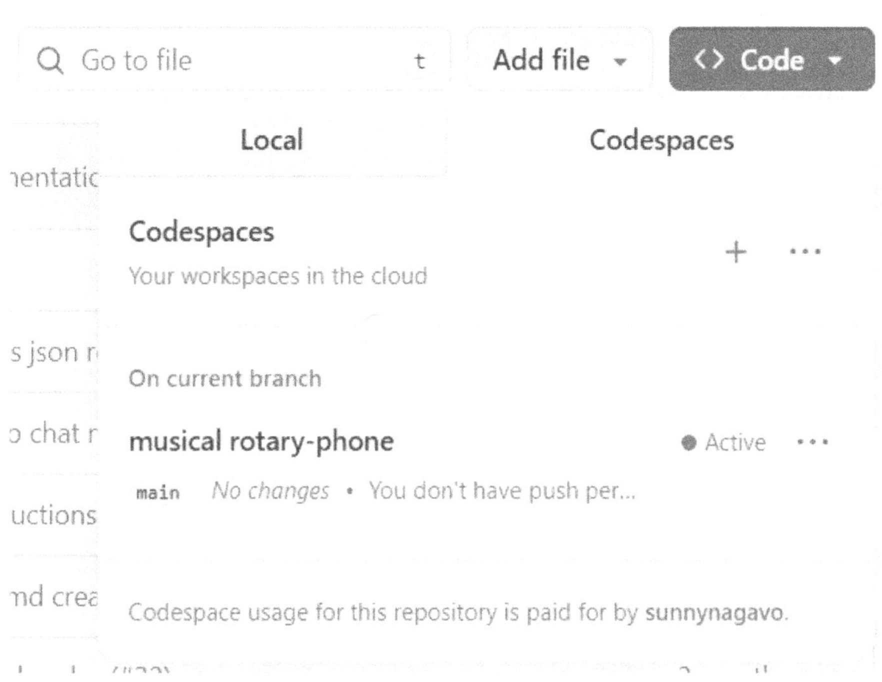

Figure 4-6. Displays the list of codespaces created by the user

By clicking on "…" you can open Codespaces either in browser or in visual studio code. It also provides you with the option to stop or delete Codespace as shown in Figure 4-7.

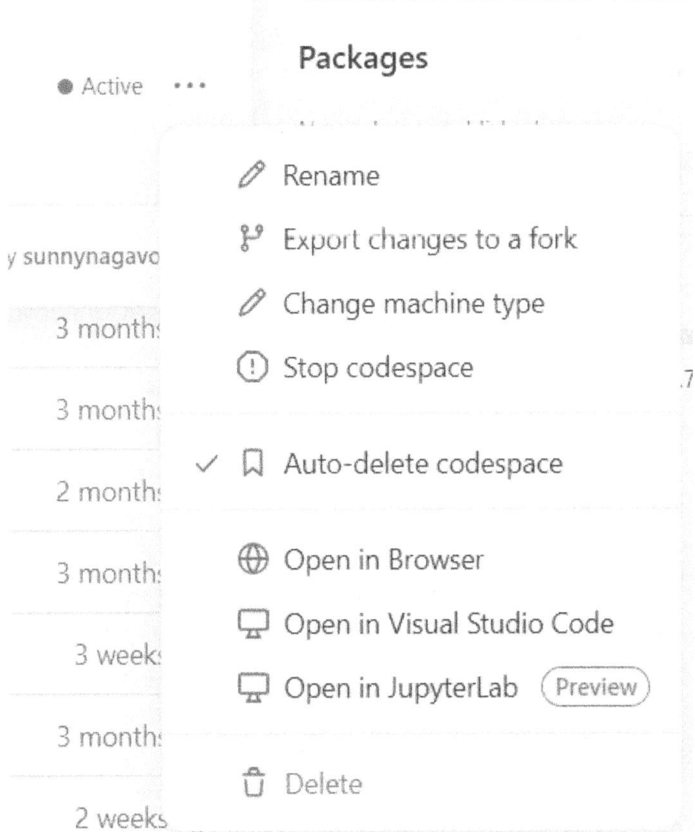

Figure 4-7. *List of options available on any Codespace*

Since Copilot Chat is available via Visual studio code extensions and Codespaces are nothing but running Visual studio code on the cloud, the integration and features of GitHub Copilot chat remain consistent across both local VS code and Codespaces. Users can expect the same chat functionalities such as asking coding-related questions, receiving explanations, generating code snippets, and debugging assistance.

Note   To avoid redundancy, refer to Chapter 3 for exploring all the features and capabilities of GitHub Copilot and GitHub Copilot Chat.

Copilot Dashboard

GitHub brought GitHub Copilot dashboard to make it easier to harness the power of AI-assisted coding in the place you already call home. The GitHub Copilot dashboard is the central hub for all AI-powered tasks on the platform. It's the first place where you will go to interact with Copilot on a broader, more project-oriented level.

To access the dashboard, click on the GitHub Icon on the right-top corner next to search button, as shown in Figure 4-8. It's part of the header, so you can see this on any page inside github.com.

Figure 4-8. *GitHub Icon is available on the top-right corner of the header*

You can also access by simply navigating to the URL "**github.com/copilot**," which opens the Copilot Dashboard as shown in Figure 4-9.

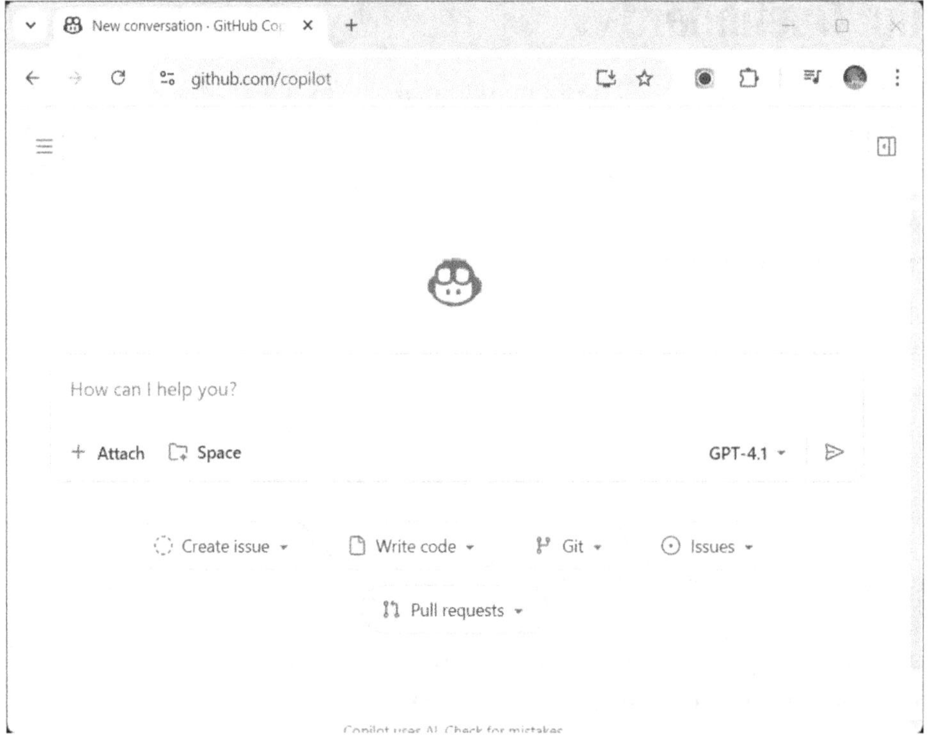

Figure 4-9. *Displays GitHub Copilot Dashboard view*

On the left side, you can see tabs to create a new chat and interact with **Agents** to delegate tasks to GitHub Coding agents to work on in the background, **Spaces** that remembers your preferences across conversations, **Spark** that quickly transforms your ideas into full stack intelligent apps, along with the list of previous chat conversations you interacted with Copilot, as shown in Figure 4-10. Most of the features are in preview mode at the time of writing this book.

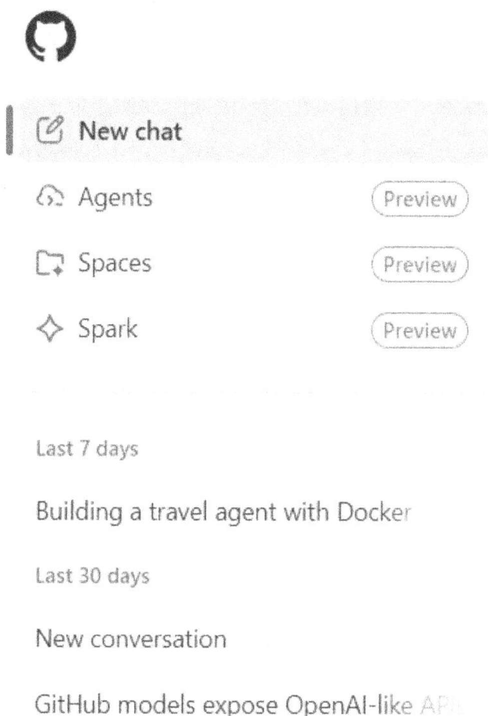

Figure 4-10. *GitHub Copilot dashboard displaying left menu options*

POINT TO NOTE

To avoid redundancy, we will not discuss each functionality within GitHub Copilot dashboard in this chapter. Even though it's a different web UI interface, there is a consistent behavior in how you interact with GitHub Copilot. You can refer to Chapter 3 for more details on different capabilities. However, in this chapter, we will dig deeper into some of the important features which are widely used and helpful to both developers and business users.

Let's investigate the input message textbox to understand some of the advanced capabilities available on Copilot dashboard.

Providing Context to GitHub Copilot

You can provide context to GitHub Copilot by clicking on **"+ Attach"** button inside the message area, which will provide you with multiple options to select from including **Repositories** or **Knowledgebases** or even **Upload from computer**.

Inside the Copilot dashboard message area, once you attach the repository that you are interested in working with, Copilot immediately responds with the below answer with examples asking "how can I assist you", as shown in Figure 4-11.

You are currently working in the GitHub repository: sunnynagavo/ACABook.

Is there anything specific you'd like to do or know about this repository? For example:

- Search for code, files, or documentation
- Review issues or pull requests
- Make code changes or open a pull request
- Draft a new GitHub issue

Let me know how I can assist you!

***Figure 4-11.** GitHub Copilot response after a repository is attached*

The chat conversation title is also created based on the repository name, which you can either rename or delete based on your needs, as shown in Figure 4-12.

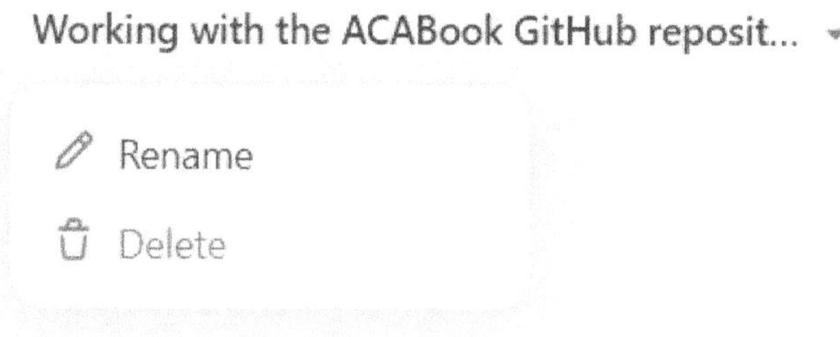

Figure 4-12. *Copilot created chat titles based on the selected repo along with options to rename and delete*

Add Extensions from Marketplace

You can install third-party extensions, which you can use directly inside the GitHub Copilot. When you type **"@"** in the input message area, Copilot will provide you with several options including extensions as shown in Figure 4-13.

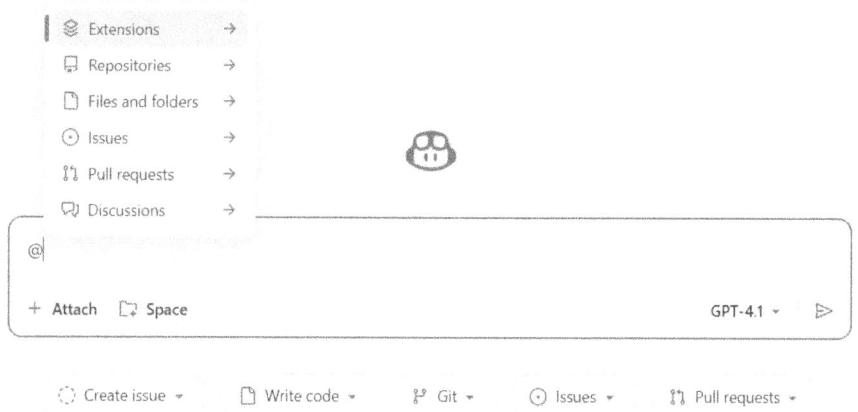

Figure 4-13. *Displays list of options when we type "@" in the input message box*

Once you click on the Extensions, it will show the list of installed extensions if you have any; otherwise, it will navigate you to marketplace page where you can see the list of available extensions to be installed (both free and paid), as shown in Figure 4-14.

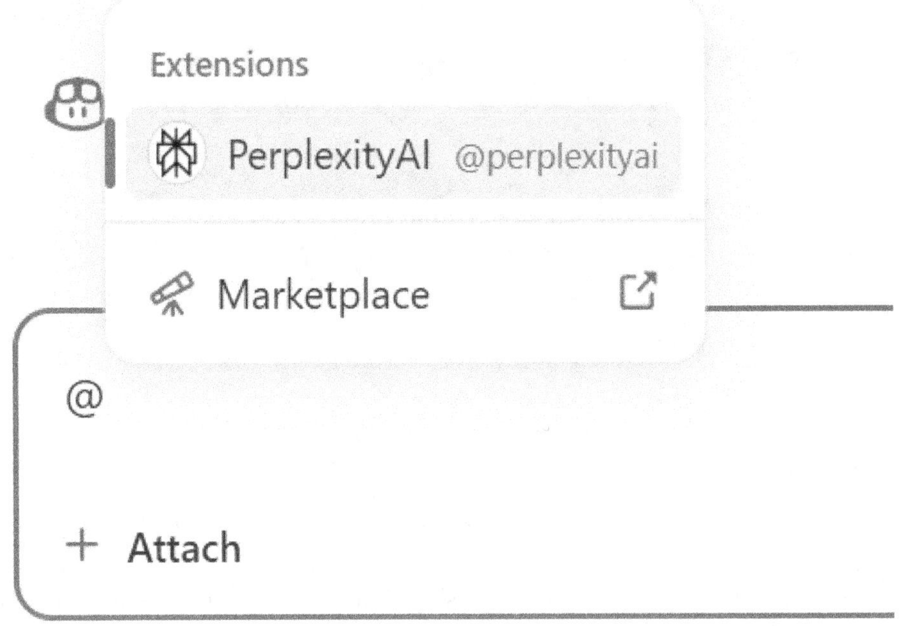

Figure 4-14. List of Copilot extensions available in the marketplace

Once you install, you can now interact with the extension directly on the chat. For example, I have installed "**PerplexityAI**" extension, and you can see when I type @ and select extensions, now I can see "**PerplexityAI**" in the options, as shown in Figure 4-15.

Figure 4-15. Shows the list of all installed extensions when user types "@"

Note   As an end user, you are responsible for setting up the pre-requisites (billing plan, permissions, authorization) required for using these third-party extensions inside GitHub Copilot.

Repository Analysis

Using GitHub Copilot directly on the web, you can ask questions about project repositories, architectural overviews, design considerations, identify any potential issues within the current repository, or even ask Copilot for any suggestions to improve.

Demonstration 1

In this demonstration, we will leverage Copilot to ask about "**dotnet/Eshop**" repository, which is a popular ecommerce repository upgraded to .NET Aspire.

Prompt: Analyze this repository and explain its architecture, identify potential issues, and suggest improvements.

Copilot returned with a response with a detailed analysis based on the repository and it provided high-level architecture overview along with strengths and possible issues/risks along with suggestions as shown in Figure 4-16.

dotnet/eShop

Analyze this repository and explain its architecture, identify potential issues, and suggest improvements

3/3

Below is an analysis based on the repository structure you provided (top level + src layout). I have not inspected individual source files, so deeper behavioral details would require a closer look at the code, configurations, and CI/CD pipelines. Still, the structure is rich enough to infer architectural intent, strengths, and likely improvement opportunities.

1. High-Level Architecture Overview

The `src` folder shows a classic modular/microservices-oriented solution for an e-commerce domain:

- Core vertical services (bounded contexts):
    - `Catalog.API` – product catalog (likely CRUD + filtering/search).
    - `Basket.API` – customer shopping basket (likely ephemeral/stateful; may use cache).
    - `Ordering.API` + `Ordering.Domain` + `Ordering.Infrastructure` – clear Domain-Driven Design layering (Domain model separated from infrastructure concerns).
    - `Identity.API` – authentication/authorization (probably issuing tokens / integrating with identity provider).
    - `Webhooks.API` + `WebhookClient` – outbound/inbound integration via callbacks.
    - `PaymentProcessor` & `OrderProcessor` – background or worker-style services handling asynchronous workflows (payments, order lifecycle).
- Cross-cutting / platform components:

Figure 4-16. *Shows an excerpt of Copilot response to a given prompt*

Like the above prompt, you can continue to chat with Copilot based on your needs or ask for more details about potential issues/risks or even ask to write code for the suggested improvements.

Intelligent Project Management with Copilot

GitHub Copilot extends its functionality beyond code and into project management. This will help us in creating and managing GitHub issues and Pull requests on any GitHub repository directly from the dashboard by leveraging Copilot.

Notice on the GitHub Copilot dashboard below the message input area; there are default options available to end users which act as quick prompts to GitHub Copilot as shown in Figure 4-17.

Figure 4-17. *List of options/prompts available to end users*

- **Create issue:** This provides prompts to create a new issue or create an issue within sub-issues.

- **Write code:** This provides prompts to create a profile readme page or work on generating code for a few quick applications like "Generating a simple calculator", "Make a pong game", etc.

- **Git:** This provides prompts to ask questions about basic Git commands, Git branching, and advanced Git commands.

- **Issues:** This provides prompts to get issues assigned to you or summarize your latest issue.

- **Pull requests:** This provides prompts to open a new pull request or summarize your latest pull request.

Note   Make sure to select the repository to provide enough context for the Copilot before using the above options. If not, Copilot will try to look at all the repositories in your account. If you navigated to Copilot dashboard by clicking on GitHub Icon on a specific repository page, Copilot will automatically attach the repository, and all your prompts will be targeted toward it.

Demonstration 2

In this demonstration, we will create an issue on the repository by leveraging GitHub Copilot.

You can either write your own custom prompt or can leverage available out of the box prompts. In this case, I went ahead and clicked on Create issue button and it sent the following prompt to Copilot.

Prompt: *First, create a new draft issue. Then ask for additional information to fill out the issue.*

Since I didn't provide any information about this issue, Copilot gave me a response with draft issue to collect necessary details before creating it as shown in Figure 4-18.

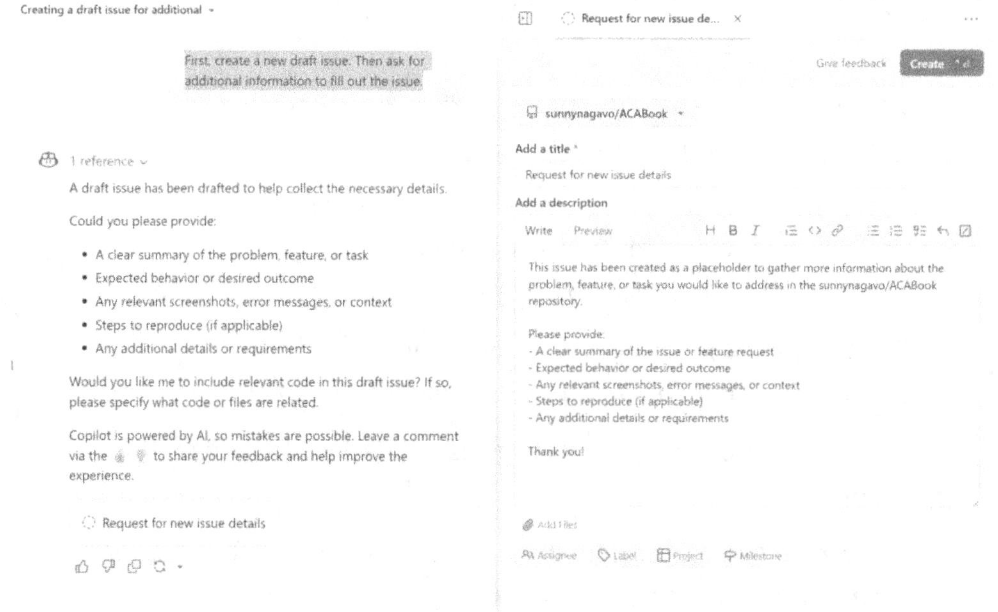

Figure 4-18. *Copilot generated a draft issue to capture more details from end user*

Instead, if I provide a custom prompt as shown below, Copilot will end up capturing the required information accordingly and it will create draft issue as shown in Figure 4-19.

Prompt: *Create an issue with the title "Need to add new chapter to the book ACA which talks about Dapr and its workflows" and assign the issue to me.*

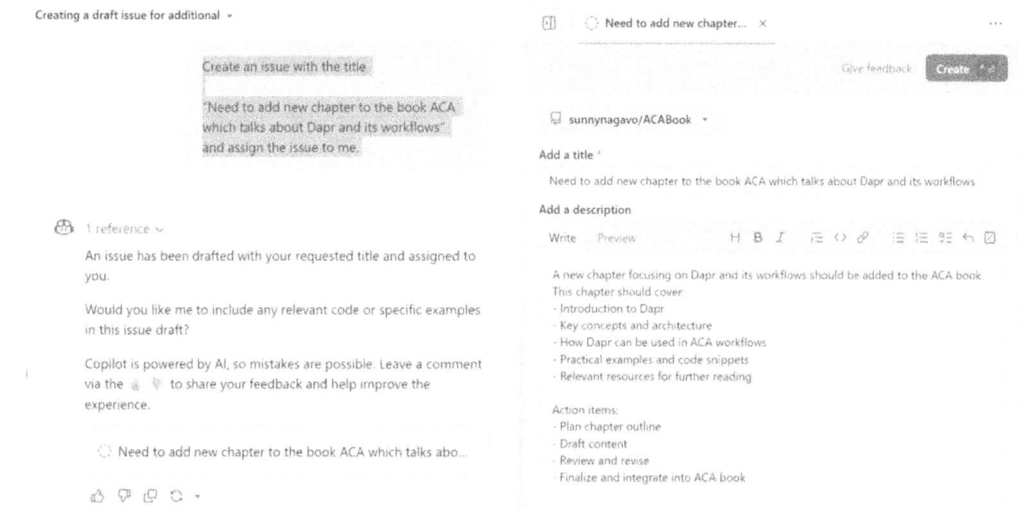

Figure 4-19. *Copilot generated draft issue with updated title and description as per the prompt*

If you observe carefully, Copilot analyzed the prompt and quickly captured details to update both Issue title as well as description to create a draft issue. As the end user, you can take necessary action to add more details to create an issue.

Demonstration 3

Prompt: List of my latest open pull requests

Since I didn't attach/mention any specific repository as context to GitHub Copilot, it went ahead and listed all the open pull requests across all the repositories under my user account as shown in Figure 4-20.

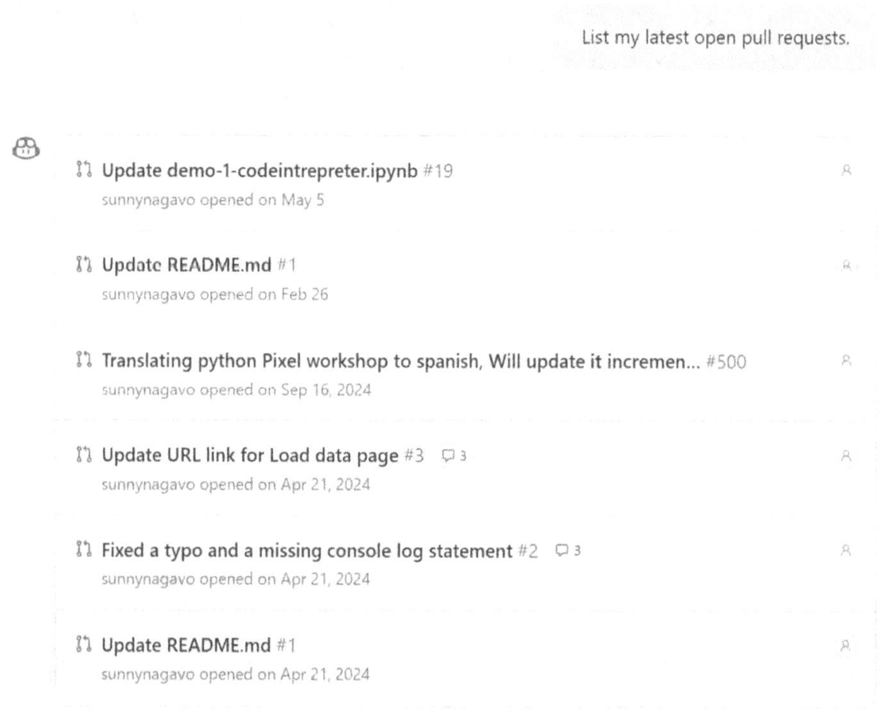

Figure 4-20. *List of all open pull requests across my repositories*

Demonstration 4

Prompt: *Search for my latest merged PR and summarize it. What was the purpose and the key changes made?*

Copilot generated the below response, where it captured the list of all merged PRs along with the summary of the most recently merged PR and the question on how to proceed next, as shown in Figure 4-21.

These results are therefore incomplete. You can view the full, up-to-date list here:
https://github.com/search?q=is%3Apr+author%3Asunnynagavo+sort%3Aupdated&type=issues

Summary of the most recently merged PR (from the retrieved set): Repository: AspireBook PR #: 11
Title: Adding MSTest project Merged at: 2025-05-26T00:34:15Z Changes: 4 files changed, 156
additions, 0 deletions (purely additive), 1 commit.

Purpose: Introduce an MSTest-based test project into the AspireBook solution to establish a formal
unit/integration testing foundation. This enables:

- A standardized test framework (MSTest) for future automated validation.
- Separation of test code from production code.
- Easier CI/CD pipeline integration for quality gates.

Key changes (inferred from metadata since the PR body was empty):

- Added a new MSTest project (likely a .csproj plus initial test class files).
- Updated the solution file to include the new test project.
- Possibly added or adjusted project/solution references so the tests can access the main
  application assemblies.
- No refactors or deletions: existing application code was left intact; this was an additive
  infrastructure enhancement.

Impact:

- Establishes baseline testing infrastructure.
- Low risk (no deletions, no modifications to existing code paths).
- Sets the stage for expanding automated test coverage going forward.

If you'd like, I can pull more details (e.g., specific file names or test class contents) or fetch newer
merged PRs beyond May 26, 2025—just let me know.

Figure 4-21. *GitHub Copilot response with details about last merged PR*

Submitting Pull Requests

The pull request (PR) is the cornerstone of modern software development. It's the key
moment where your work is shared with the team for review, feedback, and eventual
integration into the main branch. However, writing a comprehensive PR description is
always a challenge and a tedious job which is often overlooked. This is where GitHub
Copilot steps in to automate and enhance the process. You can leverage GitHub Copilot
to make code changes to your repository based on its suggestions and then ask Copilot
to even create a pull request with detailed description of the changes in the edited files.

Let's take a closer look at this with an example in Demonstration 5.

Demonstration 5

In this demonstration, we will ask GitHub Copilot to first analyze current readme file and provide an improved version. You can ask Copilot to make code suggestions too based on your requirements.

Prompt: *Make improvements in the readme file under this repository.*

Once this prompt was entered, Copilot returned with a response as shown in Figure 4-22.

Figure 4-22. *Copilot returned with a response providing improvements and asking for instructions to proceed*

Once I provided more details, Copilot went ahead and generated an improved version of Readme file for the project as per the user's request. Now we would like to ask Copilot to make necessary changes in the readme.md file and automatically create a new Pull request for these changes.

Prompt: *These changes look good. Can you incorporate them by creating a new Pull request with the changes to readme file.*

Once this prompt was entered, this will trigger a response from Copilot where it is asking for approval to create pull request as shown in Figure 4-23. In this case, Copilot is leveraging **"GitHub Copilot Coding Agent"** tool which we will discuss in depth in Chapter 5.

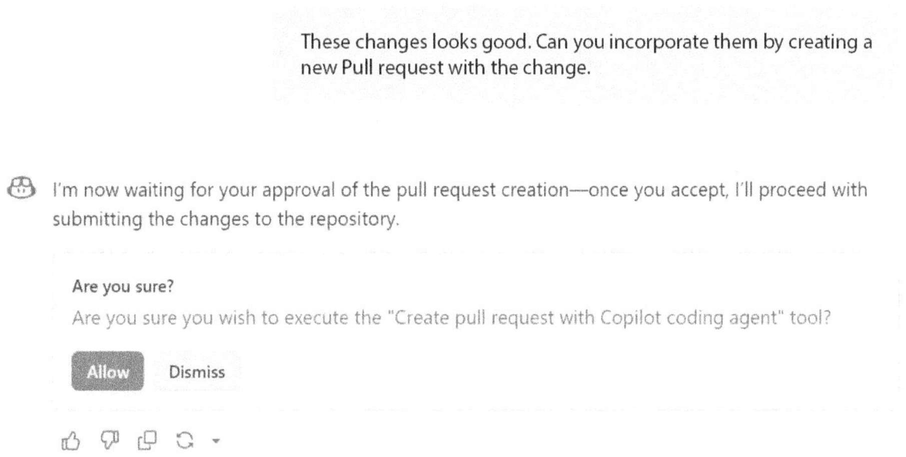

Figure 4-23. *Copilot requesting approval to leverage coding agent to complete the task*

Once I approved the request, it went ahead and created a new draft pull request with a title (WIP), which is work in progress, as shown in Figure 4-24.

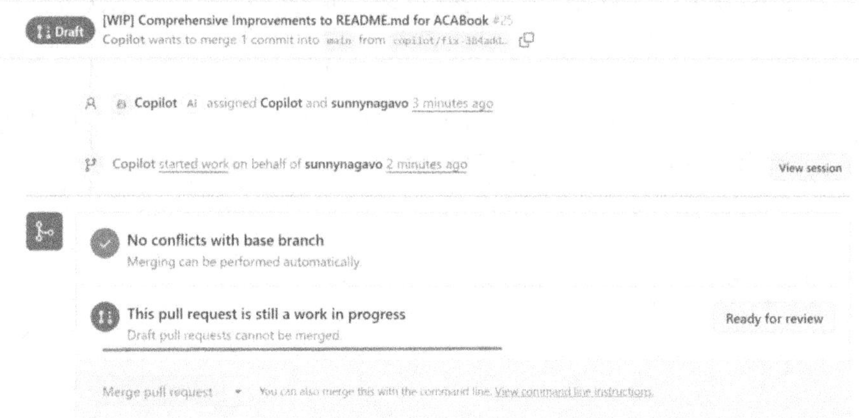

Figure 4-24. *Copilot coding agent has created WIP pull request*

Copilot coding agent will continue working on it, and it will provide an option to review once all its tasks are completed, as shown in Figure 4-25.

Figure 4-25. *Copilot coding agent is still working on the draft Pull request*

After a few minutes, Copilot coding agent has completed the work and it's now requesting user's input to review this PR, as shown in Figure 4-26.

Figure 4-26. *Copilot is requesting author to review this Pull request*

You can make changes on top of this PR if you need to and submit it to your team for approval.

Note   For approving the changes, only users who did not collaborate with Copilot will satisfy review requirements.

Demonstration 6

In this demonstration, we will ask GitHub Copilot to look at the opened pull request and provide code review comments.

You can interact with Copilot or review this pull request by creating Codespace as shown in Figure 4-27.

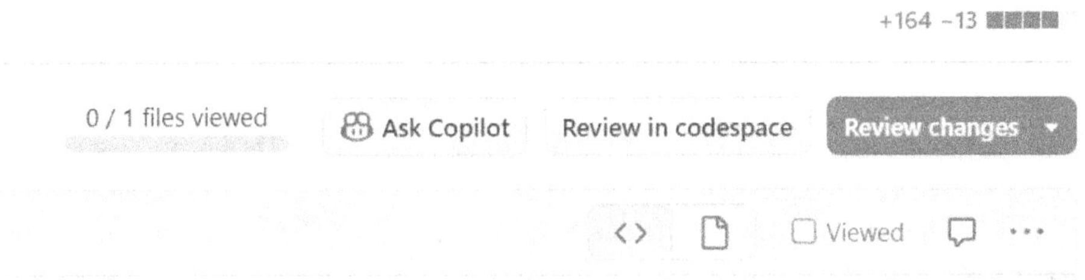

Figure 4-27. *Pull request displays options to review or interact with copilot*

Once we clicked "Review in Codespace" button, it opened a new web interface as we discussed before. Copilot returned with an approval request as shown in Figure 4-28.

Figure 4-28. Copilot returned with an approval request to read details about active PR.

Once I allowed the request, Copilot spent a few minutes to analyze the PR and provided me with a full summary of the changes along with questions to validate the readme file against the repository as shown in Figure 4-29.

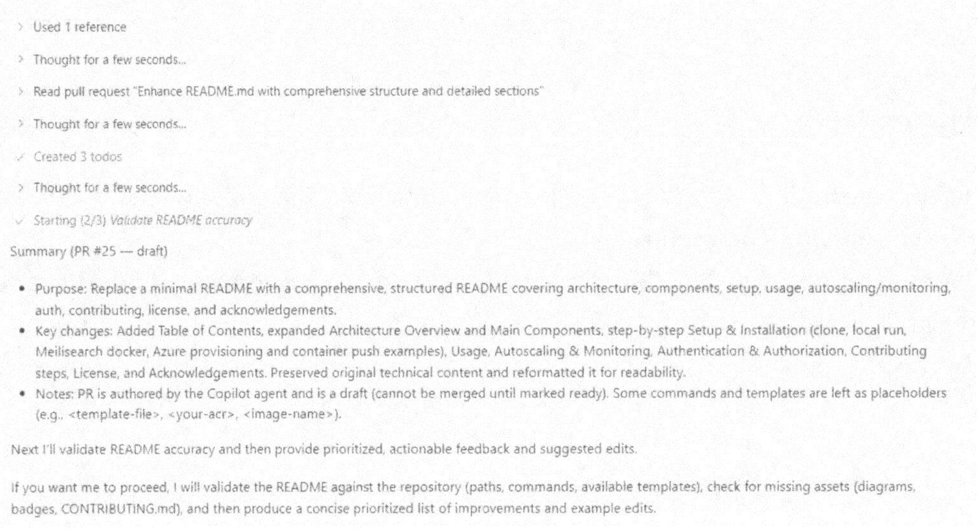

Figure 4-29. Copilot response about PR summary and asking to validate readme file accuracy

You can continue interacting with Copilot to get detailed information about reviewing the PR and provide meaningful comments or suggestions to the Author accordingly.

Q&A Session

Q4.1 What are the two ways for accessing GitHub Web editor?

The two main methods are using a keyboard shortcut or URL modification.

- **Keyboard Shortcut:** Press the period (.) key while viewing any repository page on GitHub.com to instantly launch the web editor.

- **URL Modification:** Modify the domain of any GitHub repository URL from github.com to github.dev (e.g.: `https://github.dev/github/awesome-copilot`)

Q4.2 What are the main advantages of using GitHub Copilot's web-based User interface?

The main advantages include immediate access without local development environment setup, cross-platform compatibility through any web browser, real-time collaboration capabilities, automated workflow generation, and the ability to perform complex tasks from anywhere and on any machine with internet access.

Q4.3 What is Copilot dashboard and what does it offer?

Copilot dashboard is a central hub for performing AI-powered tasks on GitHub.com. You can access it by clicking on the Copilot icon near the search bar (or navigating to URL **github.com/copilot**). It provides you with access tabs for chats, coding agents (to delegate tasks), Spaces (context collections), and Spark (for rapid prototyping). You can also manage repositories and previous conversations and attach context like repositories or documents to Copilot chats.

Q4.4 How does GitHub Copilot assist with pull request management?

GitHub Copilot can automatically generate detailed pull request descriptions based on code changes, create comprehensive review summaries for reviewers, suggest code improvements during reviews, and help maintain consistent documentation.

Q4.5 What is GitHub Spark and how does it help developers?

GitHub Spark (still in public preview) is an AI-powered tool that lets you build and deploy full-stack apps using natural language prompts. It integrates with the GitHub platform to rapidly turn ideas into deployable apps, accelerating prototyping and experimental project workflows directly inside GitHub.

Note   We will cover GitHub Spark in a case study by creating an application
to understand the platform's capabilities and how it will accelerate in creating
prototypes quickly.

Summary

In this chapter, we explored GitHub copilot's web-based capabilities demonstrating how
these powerful features transform the web UI based development experience. It allows
you to write, review, and manage code with features like intelligent code suggestions
in the web editor, chat-based repository analysis, and automated generation of pull
requests, providing meaningful code reviews and easy management of issues and tasks
directly from your web browser.

In the next chapter, we will discuss about Model Context Protocol (MCP) and how
GitHub Copilot extension running inside IDE can interact and work with various MCP
tools including GitHub MCP server, and we will also explore about GitHub coding agents
and how these help developers in transforming their ideas into quick prototypes.

CHAPTER 5

Exploring MCP and GitHub Copilot Coding Agent

In Chapter 4, we explored about leveraging GitHub Copilot's powerful features directly through GitHub.com web interface. In this chapter, you will be introduced to the Model Context Protocol (MCP) and its revolutionary impact on AI-assisted development. We will examine GitHub's official MCP server and understand how it enables seamless integration between AI applications and GitHub's ecosystem. We will also explore the emerging world of autonomous GitHub Copilot Coding Agent along with a real-world practical use case. The learning objectives for this chapter include the following:

- Understanding the Model Context Protocol (MCP) and its architecture.

- Exploring GitHub MCP server features and its tool capabilities

- Learning how to configure and use MCP servers with AI applications

- Implementing a MCP server using C# from scratch

- Understanding the security and governance aspects of MCP

- Exploring GitHub Copilot Coding Agent and its integration with development workflows

- Practical use cases to demonstrate the power of coding agents when working on development tasks

- Exploring built-in security protections when working with GitHub Copilot Coding Agent

© Naga Santhosh Reddy Vootukuri 2025
N. S. Reddy Vootukuri, *Vibe Coding with GitHub Copilot*, https://doi.org/10.1007/979-8-8688-2196-7_5

By the end of this chapter, you will master the fundamentals of MCP and have enough knowledge to create an MCP server using C# on your own. Leverage GitHub Copilot Coding Agent to transform your development workflows into a more efficient AI enhanced process. Let's embark on this journey into the future of software development!

Introduction to Model Context Protocol (MCP)

The Model Context Protocol (MCP) is an open source, open standard protocol created by Anthropic that standardizes how Large Language Models (LLMs) connect to external systems and data sources. With MCP, there is a fundamental shift in how AI applications interact with external systems. In simpler terms, think MCP is like a **"USB-C standard"** for AI applications. Like how USB-C offers a standardized way to connect your devices to various peripherals and accessories, MCP also provides a similar standard to connect AI models to different data sources and tools. Figure 5-1 shows how MCP clients hosting AI applications (LLM) can interact with other MCP servers.

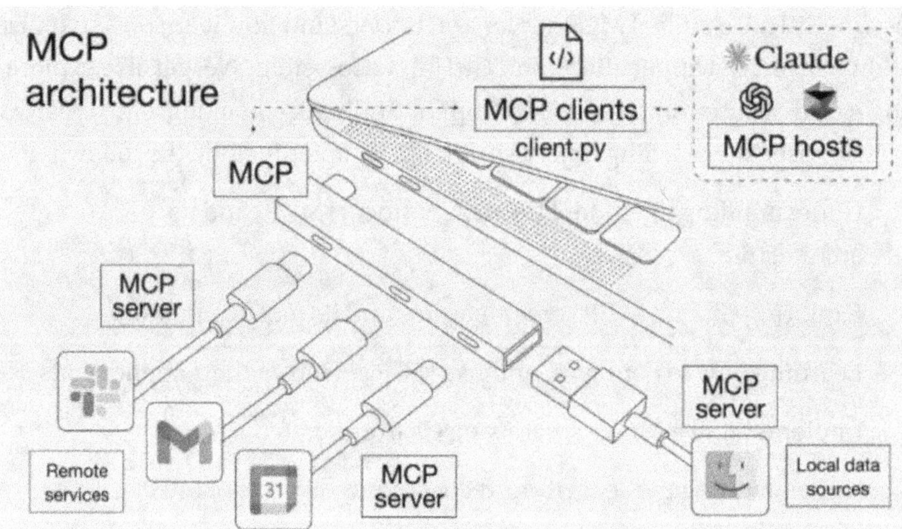

Figure 5-1. *MCP architecture depicting client server architecture*

Before MCP, connecting AI applications to external tools/APIs was extremely complicated. Imagine you have 3 different AI applications (like cursor, Claude desktop, Chatbot), and you want each one to connect to 4 different services (like GitHub, PostgreSQL db., Google drive, and Slack APIs to send messages). Without a standard way to connect, you as a developer would end up building 12 separate integrations (3 AI apps x 4 Services = 12 Integrations) wasting time, writing duplication code, and an overall frustrating development experience.

With MCP as a standard protocol, you can now create a single MCP server for each service that acts as a universal connector. Instead of building 12 separate integrations, you only need to build 4 MCP servers (one for each service). All AI applications connect to the central MCP protocol layer which then route requests to the appropriate service. Figure 5-2 depicts the integrations we need to create with and without MCP protocol.

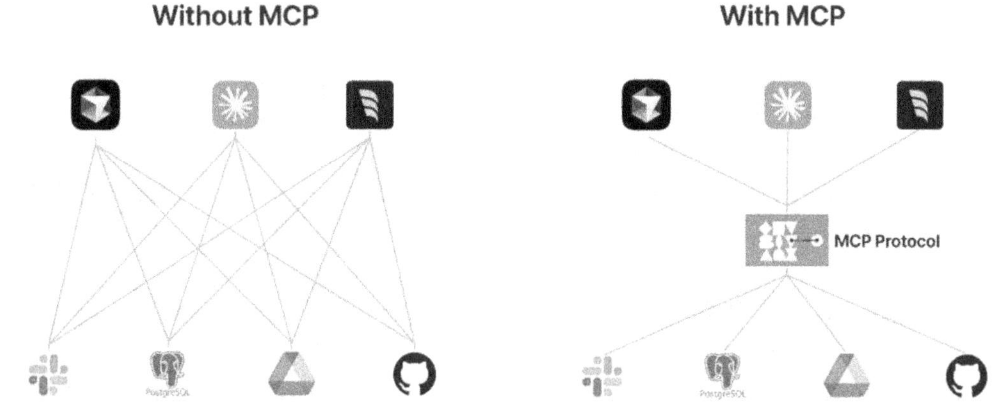

Figure 5-2. *Displays integrations with and without MCP protocol*

MCP Architecture and Core Components

The Model Context Protocol (MCP) follows client-server architecture where a host application can connect to multiple servers as shown in Figure 5-3. The MCP protocol aims to provide a universal way for AI applications to interact with external systems.

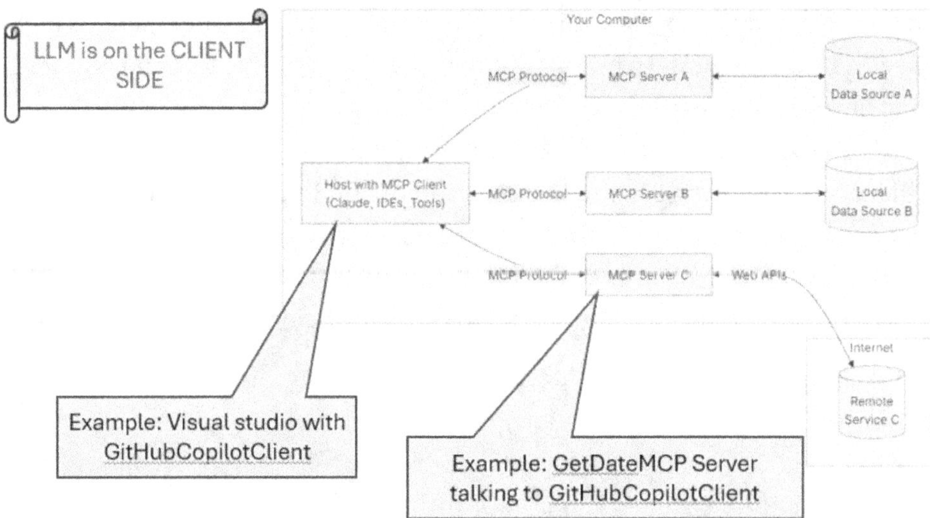

Figure 5-3. *MCP architecture with details about MCP client interacting with MCP servers via MCP protocol*

How does it work? MCP host on the left side with MCP client (e.g., Visual studio with GitHub Copilot or Claude Desktop) connects to multiple servers via MCP protocol. We provide JSON configuration files mentioning details about MCP server. Each MCP server is exposing an external tool or a data source (like local database or file system). We can also have MCP server reaching out to remote resources like APIs running on cloud.

Let's dissect and understand all the core components in a detailed way.

- **Host Application:** These are AI applications that users interact with such as Claude desktop, AI-enhanced IDEs like Visual studio, cursor or web-based LLM chat interfaces. The host application initiates connections and manages the overall user experience.

- **MCP Client:** The MCP client handles connections with MCP servers and translates between Host's requirements and the Model context protocol. These are integrated within the host applications. MCP Client maintains 1:1 connection with MCP servers. (e.g., GitHub Copilot within Visual studio acts as an MCP client, where we can connect to multiple MCP servers using JSON configuration files).

- **MCP Server:** These can be standalone programs or APIs that expose specific functionality or data resources to AI applications through the MCP protocol. Each MCP server typically focuses on a specific integration such as connecting to GitHub for repository access, PostgreSQL for database operations or file systems, etc.

- **MCP Protocol:** It is an open source standard that defines a secure, two-way communication framework for AI systems to interact with external systems.

- **Prompts:** Prompts are reusable templates that help in interactions with Large Language Models (LLMs). Within these predefined templates, it can also support variable substitutions.

- **Transport layer:** The Communication mechanism between clients and servers supports two primary methods.

  - **STDIO (standard input/output):** Mainly used for local integrations where both server and clients run in the same environment. Messages are sent synchronously over the application's standard input and output streams.

  - **HTTP + SSE (server-sent events):** Mainly used for enabling remote connections where MCP server is a web service running separately where HTTP is used for client initial requests and SSE (server-sent events) utilized for server responses allowing efficient and real-time streaming.

Note JSON-RPC 2.0   is used as the underlying base message standard for all communications between MCP clients and servers, providing a structured format for requests, responses, and notifications.

What can MCP server expose? MCP servers expose three main types of capabilities, as shown in Figure 5-4.

- **Tools:** These are the functions that Large Language Models (LLMs) can call into to perform specific actions. For example, Weather service API, database query functions, etc. Tools enable AI models to take actions in the external world.

- **Resources:** These are the data sources that LLMs can access, like GET endpoints in a REST API. These data sources act as a knowledge base for LLMs.

- **Prompts:** These are predefined templates that can be consumed from LLMs, which help in optimizing the use of tools or resources.

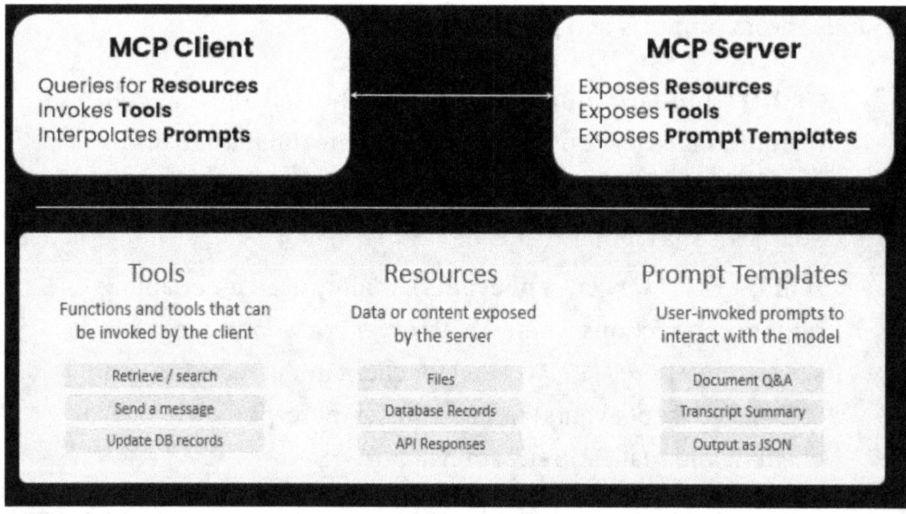

Figure 5-4. *Shows MCP server's capabilities along with examples for each capability (courtesy from Microsoft)*

GitHub Official MCP Server

GitHub team released an official MCP sever that implements the Model Context Protocol, which allows AI tools and applications to easily interact with GitHub's ecosystem. Using GitHub MCP server, we can now directly interact with GitHub Repositories, pull requests automation, and manage GitHub Issues and GitHub Actions in a safe and secure manner.

For more details about GitHub MCP server, refer to the official GitHub MCP server link at `https://github.com/github/github-mcp-server`.

You can configure GitHub MCP server in two ways:

Local GitHub MCP Server: Deployed within your organization's infrastructure for enhanced security and control. We need Docker installed and running on your system along with GitHub personal access token (PAT) with proper permissions to access GitHub APIs.

You can either do a one-click installation or manually configure it in VS by following the steps below.

Click on the Tools button inside GitHub Copilot Agent mode chat window as shown in Figure 5-5.

Figure 5-5. *GitHub Copilot Agent mode with tools button*

You can click on edit to open the MCP.JSON settings file to enter the JSON configuration as shown below.

```
{
  "inputs": [
    {
      "type": "promptString",
      "id": "github_token",
      "description": "GitHub Personal Access Token",
      "password": true
    }
  ],
  "servers": {
    "github": {
      "command": "docker",
```

```
      "args": [
        "run",
        "-i",
        "--rm",
        "-e",
        "GITHUB_PERSONAL_ACCESS_TOKEN",
        "ghcr.io/github/github-mcp-server"
      ],
      "env": {
        "GITHUB_PERSONAL_ACCESS_TOKEN": "${input:github_token}"
      }
    }
  }
}
```

You need to first enter details about the required fields by clicking on the link **"Input required"** as shown in Figure 5-6.

```
        ],
    ⚠ S  This server requires user input before it can be activated.
       ⚠ Input required | Inputs
      "github": {
        "command": "docker",
        "args": [
          "run",
          "-i",
          "--rm",
          "-e",
          "GITHUB_PERSONAL_ACCESS_TOKEN",
          "ghcr.io/github/github-mcp-server"
        ],
        "env": {
          "GITHUB_PERSONAL_ACCESS_TOKEN": "${input:github_token}"
        }
      }
    }
```

Figure 5-6. *Shows Input required link to enter the GitHub PAT*

A new window to enter the GitHub Personal Access Token (PAT) will be opened as shown in Figure 5-7.

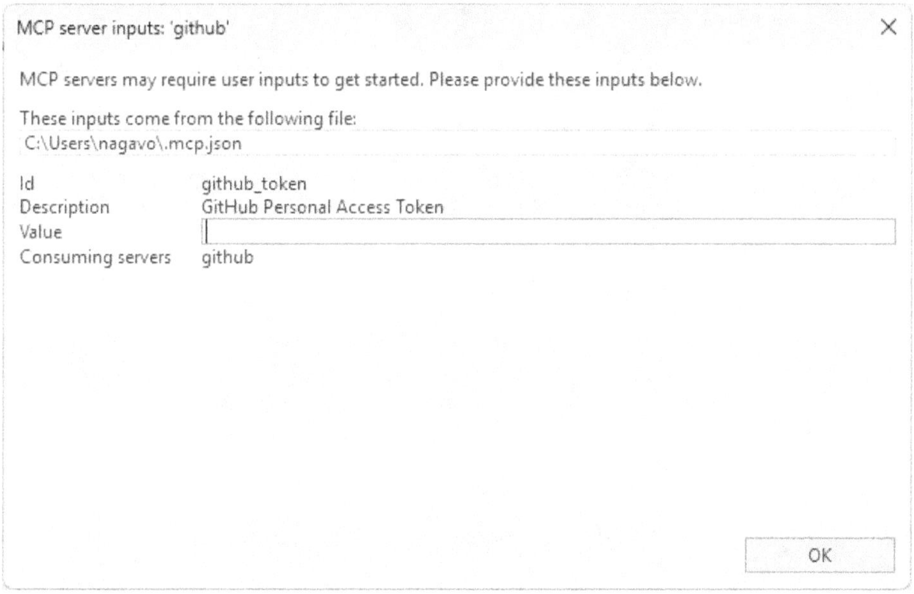

Figure 5-7. *Displays text box to enter GitHub PAT*

Once you enter PAT, make sure docker is installed and running on your local machine. You will now see GitHub MCP server running as shown in Figure 5-8.

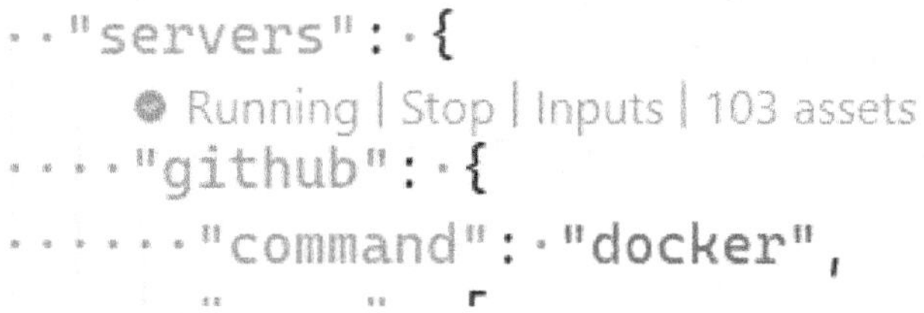

Figure 5-8. *Displays GitHub MCP server running locally*

We can also see the list of tools that are available under GitHub MCP server when you click on the tools button as shown in Figure 5-9. It shows there are 96 tools inside the GitHub MCP server, and we can filter the tools to select or unselect accordingly.

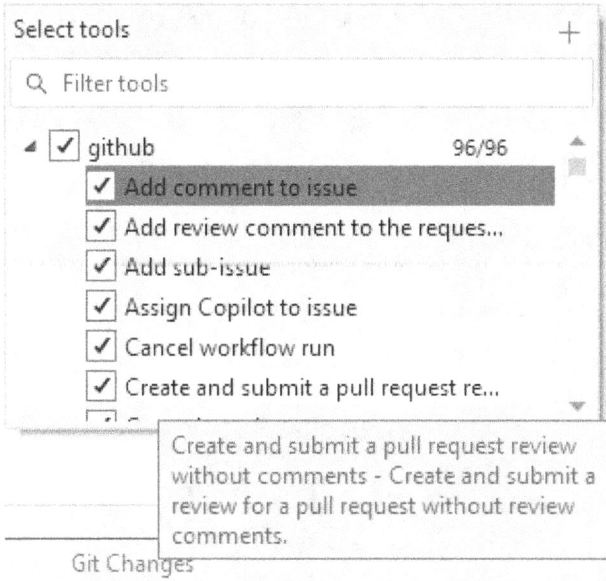

Figure 5-9. *Displays the list of tools available under GitHub MCP Server*

POINT TO NOTE

For creating a GitHub Personal Access token, visit Developer settings ➤ PAT ➤ Fine-grained tokens and click on "Generate New Token" or simply navigate to the link `https://github.com/settings/personal-access-tokens/new` *to create a new token. Provide details about name, expiration date, and select the list of repositories for which you want the token to access along with necessary permissions to grant.*

Remote GitHub MCP Server: The GitHub remote MCP server is fully hosted by GitHub, which is always an up-to-date implementation of MCP. This was released in August 2025 and is currently in public preview at the time of writing this book. We can install remote server by one-click installation inside VS or VS code, or by opening command palette inside VS Code and run **"GitHub MCP: Install remote server",** follow prompts to complete OAuth setup to connect to your GitHub Account. Restart the server to finish setup.

Another way is to set up using MCP.JSON configuration file with the configuration as shown below.

```
{
  "mcpServers": {
    "github": {
      "type": "http/sse",
      "url": "https://api.githubcopilot.com/mcp/",
      "auth": {
        "type": "oauth",
        "scopes": ["copilot_read"]
      },
      "tools": [
        // List of tools provided by the GitHub MCP server, e.g.,
        // "get_issue_details",
        // "get_pull_request_details",
        // "search_code"
      ]
    }
  }
}
```

Note   With the help of GitHub's remote-managed MCP server, we can now eliminate the local infrastructure issues; no need to manage Docker and no need to worry about expiring access tokens. Point your IDE or agent host to `https://api.githubcopilot.com/mcp/` and authenticate once with OAuth, and GitHub handles the rest.

GitHub MCP Server Capabilities

GitHub MCP server provides comprehensive toolsets organized by functionality. Table 5-1 shows some of the frequently used ones ranging from Repository management to GitHub Issues management to Pull request management. We have 96 tools available as of today(September 29, 2025) inside GitHub MCP server.

Table 5-1. *Displays an excerpt of Capabilities/Tools from GitHub MCP server*

Capability	Description
search_repositories	Search for repositories across GitHub
create_repository	Create new repositories
get_file_contents	Retrieve file contents from repositories
create_or_update_file	Modify single files in repositories
push_files	Commit multiple file changes at once
create_branch	Create new branches in repositories
get_issue	Retrieve issue details by specifying owner, repository, and issue number
create_issue	Create new issues with customizable title, body, assignees, and labels
list_issues	List and filter repository issues with various criteria
update_issue	Update existing issues
search_issues	Search for issues across GitHub
add_issue_comment	Add comments to existing issues
get_pull_request	Retrieve PR details
create_pull_request	Create new pull requests
list_pull_requests	List and filter repository PRs
merge_pull_request	Merge open pull requests
get_pull_request_files	Retrieve files changed in a PR
update_pull_request_ branch	Update a PR branch with latest changes from base

Demonstration 1

In this demonstration, let's use GitHub MCP server to create a GitHub Issue as shown in Figure 5-10.

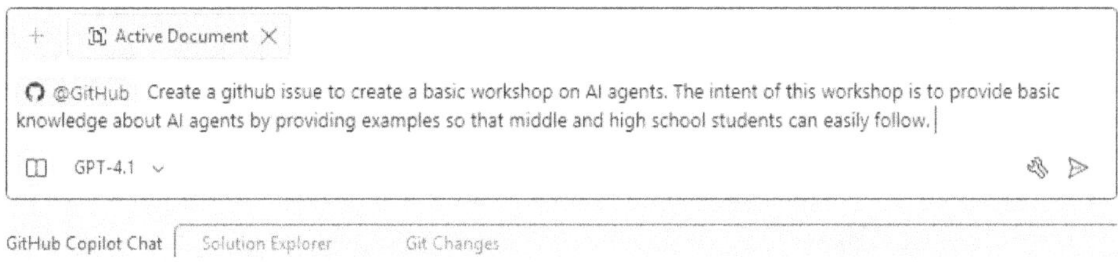

Figure 5-10. *Displays prompt GitHub Copilot to create a GitHub Issue*

GitHub Copilot responded with an approval to execute **"Create_issue"** function to create the GitHub Issue as shown in Figure 5-11.

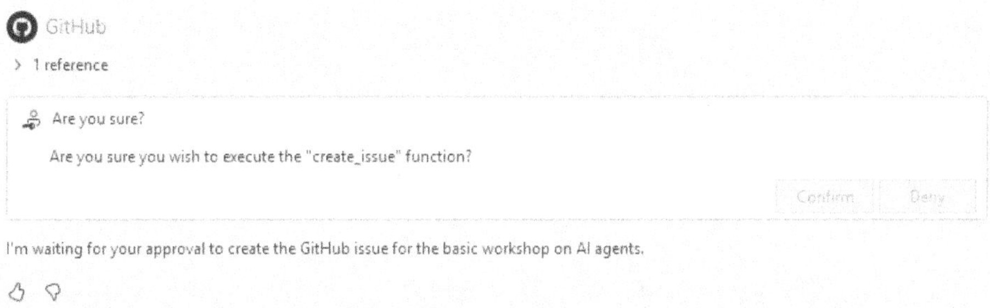

Figure 5-11. *GitHub Copilot responded with a confirmation message to execute "Create_issue" function*

Once we click "confirm" button, GitHub Copilot leverages GitHub MCP server to successfully create an issue and provides a link to track it when it's ready, as shown in Figure 5-12.

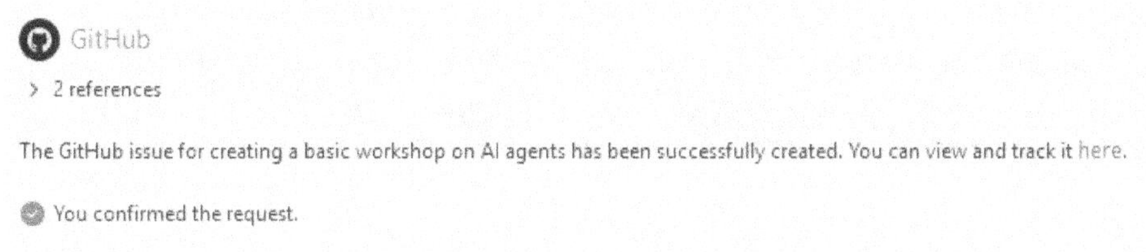

Figure 5-12. *GitHub Copilot responded with a link after successfully creating GitHub Issue*

You can navigate by clicking on the link to verify the details of the newly created GitHub Issue by GitHub Copilot as shown in Figure 5-13.

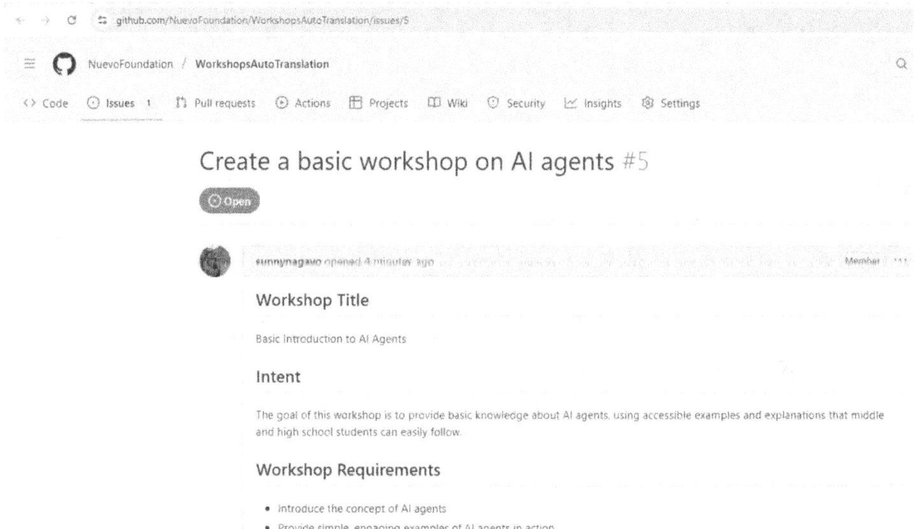

Figure 5-13. *GitHub Issue was created by GitHub Copilot using GitHub MCP server*

You can see the Issue name along with the intent and workshop requirements as per my prompt. If you need to make any modifications or corrections, you can edit the GitHub issue exactly how you would do it when manually creating GitHub Issues.

POINT TO NOTE

Demonstration 1 is just one example to leverage GitHub MCP server; however, you can use GitHub MCP server, which has 96 tools inside it, with various workflows ranging from creating GitHub Issues to creating repositories and creating Pull request to running GitHub Actions. Based on your use case, provide right prompt to the GitHub Copilot.

How to Build an MCP Server from Scratch

The Model Context Protocol (MCP) provides official Software Development kits (SDKs) for multiple languages like Java, C#, Typescript, Python, Kotlin, Swift, and Rust.

Refer to `https://github.com/modelcontextprotocol/csharp-sdk` for more details about C# SDK.

Using the above SDK, developers can now build both servers and clients that leverage this protocol. Leveraging this SDK will simplify the implementation process, allowing you to focus on your application features instead of complexities in protocol handling. SDK provides support in consuming MCP servers and also creating robust client applications that can interact with MCP servers.

Demonstration 2

In this demonstration, we will explore how to use C# SDK to create our own MCP server and client applications. **Example**: We will create a Weather MCP Server that will provide accurate weather information when we provide state details as parameter.

Let's start by creating MCP server. Let's use default Console application template from Visual Studio or simply run the below command in the terminal to create a new console application.

```
dotnet new console -n WeatherMCPServer
```

To get started, install the required NuGet Packages as shown below.

```
dotnet add package ModelContextProtocol --prerelease
dotnet add package Microsoft.Extensions.Hosting
```

- **ModelContextProtocol:** Adds the C# MCP SDK so that we can build or consume MCP clients/servers and expose the tools/resources for LLMs workflows.

- **Microsoft.Extensions.Hosting:** This package provides generic host, dependency injections, configuration, and lifetime management needed to run MCP server as a long-running service.

Let's update **Program.cs file** to create our weather MCP server. The code below is to configure STDIO server transport and inform our server to search for all the Tools available from the running assembly.

```
using Microsoft.Extensions.DependencyInjection;
using Microsoft.Extensions.Hosting;
using Microsoft.Extensions.Logging;
```

```
namespace WeatherMCPServer
{
    internal class Program
    {
        public static async Task Main(string[] args)
        {
            var builder = Host.CreateApplicationBuilder(args);
            builder.Logging.AddConsole(consoleLogOptions =>
            {
                // Configure all logs to go to stderr
                consoleLogOptions.LogToStandardErrorThreshold =
                LogLevel.Trace;
            });

            builder.Services
                .AddMcpServer()
                .WithStdioServerTransport()
                .WithToolsFromAssembly();

            await builder.Build().RunAsync();
        }
    }
}
```

For creating Weather MCP server tools, let's create a new file named "WeatherTools" where it will contain functions that are exposed as "**Tools**". Below code shows an excerpt from the WeatherTools.cs file, which shows how we add attributes to the class and methods.

```
[McpServerToolType]
public static class WeatherTools
{
    [McpServerTool(Name = "getWeatherByCountry"), Description("Gets current
    weather (temp C, humidity %, wind m/s) for the specified country
    name.")]
```

```csharp
public static async Task<string> GetWeatherByCountryAsync(
    HttpClient httpClient,
    [Description("Country name, e.g. 'France', 'India', 'United
    States'")] string country,
    CancellationToken cancellationToken)
    => await GetWeatherAsync(httpClient, country, "country",
    cancellationToken);

[McpServerTool(Name = "getWeatherByState"), Description("Gets current
weather (temp C, humidity %, wind m/s) for the specified state / region
name.")]
public static async Task<string> GetWeatherByStateAsync(
    HttpClient httpClient,
    [Description("State or region name, e.g. 'California',
    'Queensland', 'Bavaria'")] string state,
    CancellationToken cancellationToken)
    => await GetWeatherAsync(httpClient, state, "state",
    cancellationToken);
}
```

From the startup code, "WithToolsFromAssembly" will scan the assembly for all classes marked with attribute "McpServerToolType" and register all the methods with "McpServerTool" attribute. We can add name and description as parameters to this attribute which is then fed into any client connecting to the server. This description is crucial and helps LLMs to determine which tool to invoke.

Note   Implementation of GetWeatherAsync is not important for this demonstration; you can add simple switch case hardcoded values for different states/countries or implement by talking to external weather APIs.

Now that we have created our first MCP server, let's see how to consume it in our GitHub Copilot. To run project locally, add the below JSON configuration in our mcp. schema.json file under "**..\\..\\program%20files\\microsoft%20visual%20studio\\2022\\ preview\\common7\\ide\\extensions\\microsoft\\copilot\\mcp.schema.json**" or in your user settings.

```
{
    "inputs": [],
    "servers": {
        " WeatherMCP ": {
            "type": "stdio",
            "command": "dotnet",
            "args": [
                "run",
                "--project",
                " C:\\source\\repos\\WeatherMCPServer\\WeatherMCPServer.
                csproj "
            ]
        }
    }
}
```

Note   "C:\\source\\repos\\WeatherMCPServer\\WeatherMCPServer.csproj" is the location where your Weather MCP project file exists.

Make sure to restart the newly added MCP server to show it's in "Running" state as shown in Figure 5-14.

Figure 5-14. *Displays "Running" state of newly added WeatherMCP server*

If you open the GitHub Copilot tools window, you can see the **WeatherMCP** server along with the list of **Tools(functions)** as shown in Figure 5-15.

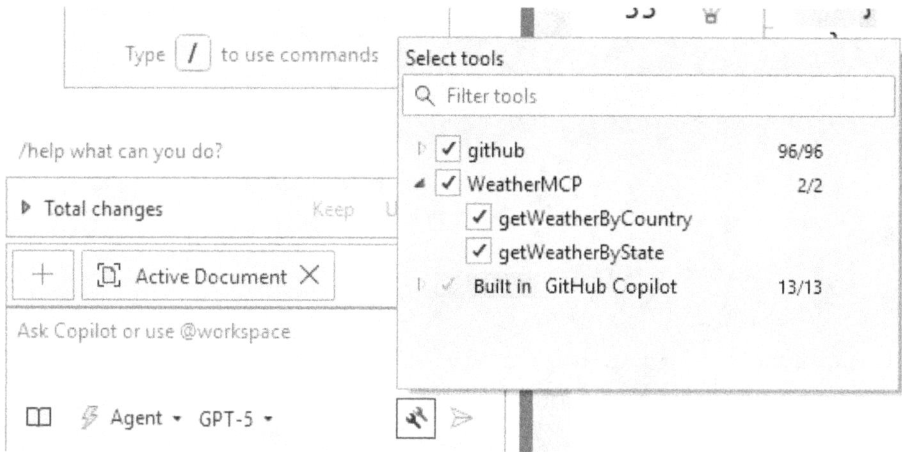

Figure 5-15. *Shows the MCP server and its Tools(functions) to be selected in agent mode*

Now that the MCP server is set up properly, let's ask GitHub Copilot in Agent mode to retrieve current weather information for Seattle as shown in Figure 5-16.

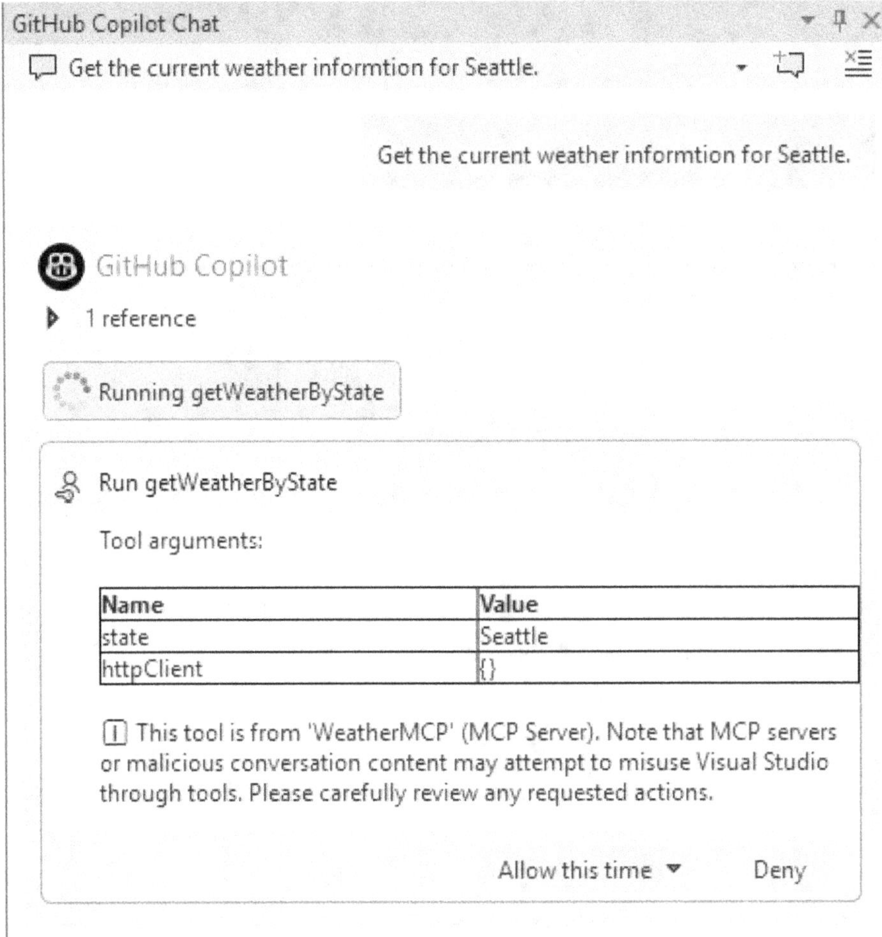

Figure 5-16. *Copilot responded with a confirmation message using right tool*

Once you confirm, GitHub Copilot will invoke your locally created function (Tool), in this case "**getWeatherByState**" from the Weather MCP server, and return the response from executing the function.

Security Practices in Model Context Protocol (MCP)

Model Context Protocol (MCP) is gaining a lot of attention, and when reaping the benefits of flexibility and interoperability, we should also be careful about significant safety and security challenges. Why? Since we expose AI models with full access to tools and data sources via MCP, it expands the applications' attack surface. Without following best practices, you can expose sensitive information or allow remote code execution. Hence, when implementing MCP in your applications, follow these security best practices:

1. **Defend Against Prompt Injection Attacks:** Be cautious that malicious instructions can be hidden in external content like emails, web pages, or PDFs. When AI reads that content, it may interpret those hidden instructions and can perform unintended actions, data leaks, or harmful behavior. Implement content filtering and use tools like Microsoft's prompt shields for detection.

2. **Prevent Tool Poisoning:** Since LLMs rely on tool metadata to decide which tools to call, attackers can tamper with tool descriptions or parameters to sneak in dangerous behavior. This is especially risky in hosted environments where tools can be changed after user approval.

3. **Implement Proper Token Management:** Never allow token pass-through where clients pass their tokens directly to downstream resources. This is explicitly forbidden in MCP specs as it bypasses security controls and breaks trust boundaries. Only accept tokens issued specifically for your MCP server.

4. **Use External Identity Providers:** Authentication was a big issue, and early this year in April 2025, MCP servers can delegate authentication to external providers like Microsoft Entra ID instead of rolling your own OAuth 2.0 server. Leverage tools like API Management and official MCP security guides for best practices.

5. **Apply Least-Privilege Access:** MCP servers often access sensitive data but ensure they only get the minimum access. For example, a server meant for sales data shouldn't read all enterprise files. Use Role-based access control (RBAC), audit roles regularly, and review permissions frequently.

6. **Secure Your Supply Chain:** Your AI supply chain includes models, embeddings, APIs, and context providers – not just code. Verify sources, use secure deployment pipelines, scan for vulnerabilities, and monitor for changes continuously using tools like GitHub Advanced Security, Azure DevOps, and CodeQL.

7. **Strengthen Foundation Security:** MCP inherits your environment's existing security posture. Follow secure coding practices (OWASP Top 10 and OWASP for LLMs), harden servers with multifactor authentication, patch regularly, enable comprehensive logging and monitoring, and design with zero trust architecture.

8. **Deploy Advanced Protection:** Use Microsoft's Prompt Shields which provides detection and filtering of malicious inputs, spotlighting to distinguish system instructions from external text, delimiters for trusted vs. untrusted data marking, and continuous security updates integrated with Azure Content Safety.

GitHub Copilot Coding Agent

GitHub team introduced a revolutionary tool aka Coding Agent which can work on coding tasks inside your GitHub workflow. You can delegate your open issues to GitHub Copilot Coding Agent which can write, run, and test code in the background. You can assign issues to Coding Agent from VS Code, GitHub CLI, GitHub Mobile, or directly from GitHub.com. Unlike traditional AI code assistants, Coding Agent can

- Work in isolation on completing assigned task without constant human guidance

- Identify the appropriate files and make multiple changes across different files

- Write, test, and validate code thoroughly before submitting changes

- Create Pull Requests with detailed description and document entire changes made inside PR as per the instructions provided in the task.

How Coding Agent Works

Whenever a GitHub issue is directly assigned to a Coding Agent, the agent analyzes your codebase, identifies all the appropriate files to modify or create new files if necessary, and aligns with your project's coding style and patterns to generate code. These are the detailed steps Coding Agent performs once you assign an issue:

- Ingests context, looks into code layout, build systems, tests and workflows to understand the system.

- Plans and creates multiple steps based on the task.

- Executes in a secure isolated environment

- Corrects and iterates via code review comments.

- Opens a draft pull request in Work In progress [WIP] state to later publish it.

The Coding Agent is built with safety in mind and makes sure to route all the changes through code reviews before reaching anything to production. GitHub Coding Agent does the below things by default:

- The person who asked Coding Agent to open a pull request cannot approve it ensuring that "required reviews" policy is strictly enforced.

- Agent's internet access is restricted to a configurable list of trusted destinations.

- The Agent can only push code to the branches it created, keeping other branches safe and secure.

- GitHub Actions won't be run automatically without your approval, which means you can spot-check agent's code before running them.

Demonstration 3

In this demonstration, let's assign a task directly using Agent tasks window from GitHub.com.

Navigate to the GitHub repository where you want to assign a task to coding agent. Click on Agent tasks button to open a window, where you would like to upgrade an existing project to latest dotnet as the project was using older dotnet runtime (7.0), which is out of support as shown in Figure 5-17.

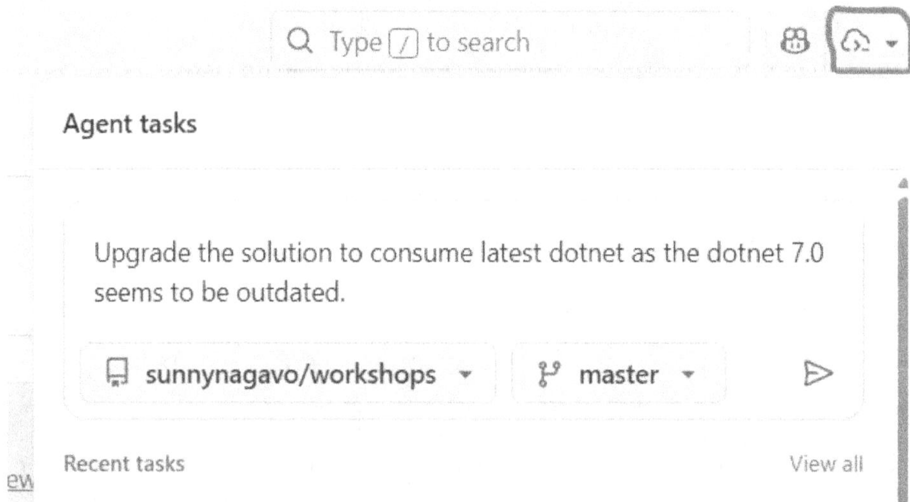

Figure 5-17. Shows Agent tasks window to assign a task to coding agent

Enter the task details and hit **submit** button to start the task. It will start with creating the task as shown in Figure 5-18.

Figure 5-18. Displays Creating task message

Once task is created, a WIP (work in progress) draft PR gets created as shown in Figure 5-19.

Agent tasks

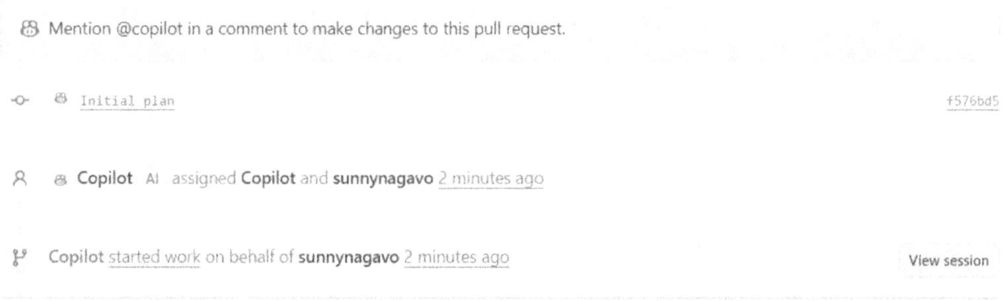

Figure 5-19. *Displays currently working tasks under the "Recent tasks" section*

If we navigate into the PR, we can see how Copilot is working through the given task. For more details on how Copilot is implementing the changes, you can click on **"view session"** button as shown in Figure 5-20.

Figure 5-20. *Copilot displays "View Session" button to display more details about the implementation*

A new page is opened with more detailed steps on what GitHub Copilot Coding Agent is working on as shown in Figure 5-21. At any given point in time you can click on "Stop Session" button on the top to stop the Agent execution.

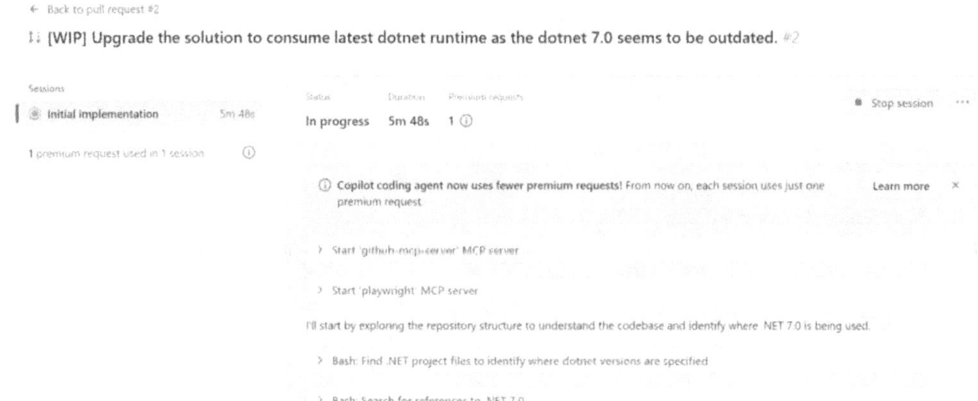

Figure 5-21. *Displays each step performed by GitHub Copilot Coding Agent*

Once GitHub Copilot Coding Agent finishes the task, you can see the message about the upgrade is complete and it also provides a detailed summary of the changes made by the Agent, as shown in Figure 5-22.

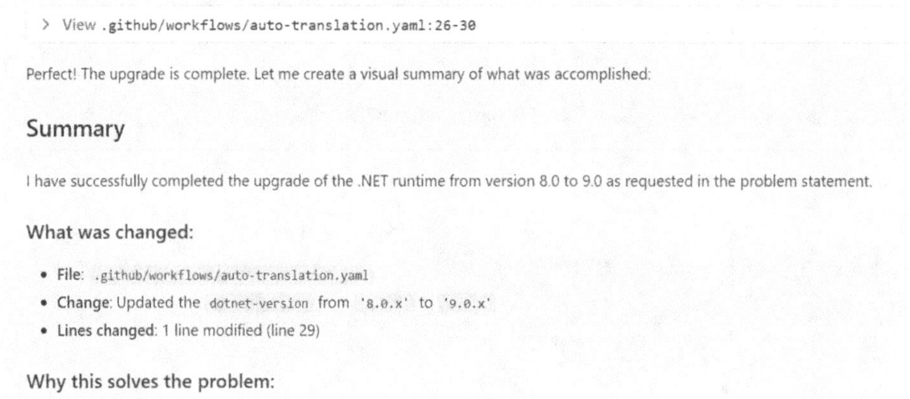

Figure 5-22. *Displays summary of the changes made by Copilot Coding Agent*

Now the Coding Agent has completed the task, and the PR is ready for reviewing as shown in Figure 5-23.

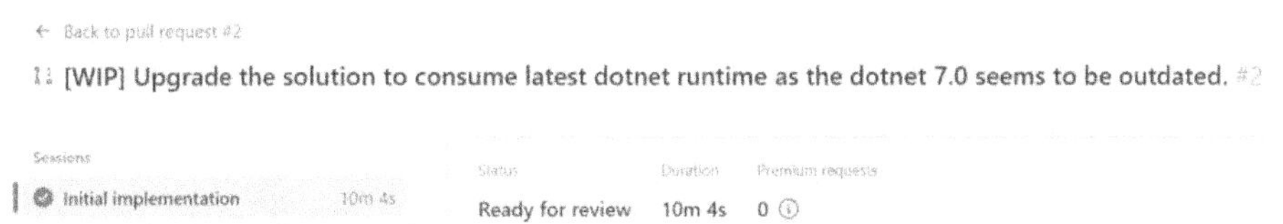

Figure 5-23. *Copilot shows initial implementation is completed*

Once we navigate back to the PR, the [WIP] (work in progress) text was removed and Copilot updated with detailed description about the overview of the change, why this change was needed along with testing, and the impact of the changes as shown in Figure 5-24.

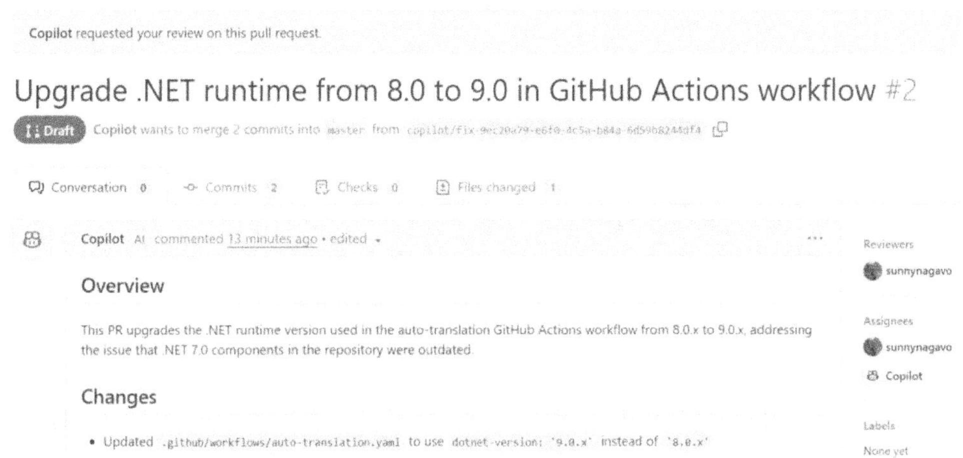

Figure 5-24. *Updated Pull request with modified title and detailed description of changes*

If you observe, Copilot has only upgraded GitHub Actions .yaml file; however, my intent was to upgrade all the projects within the solution. This is a good example to show as an end user your responsibility to verify the outcome and provide proper feedback via PR comments to the Copilot.

I went ahead and provided feedback on the same PR as a comment to Copilot as shown in Figure 5-25. Copilot looked at it and started work on my behalf.

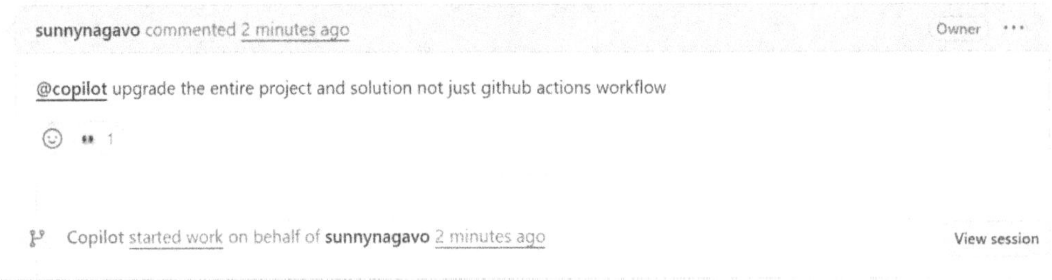

sunnynagavo commented 2 minutes ago   Owner   • • •

@copilot upgrade the entire project and solution not just github actions workflow

☺ 👀 1

Copilot started work on behalf of sunnynagavo 2 minutes ago   View session

Figure 5-25. *Copilot started working on a code comment*

At this point, Copilot detected the lists of projects that need an upgrade, as shown in Figure 5-26.

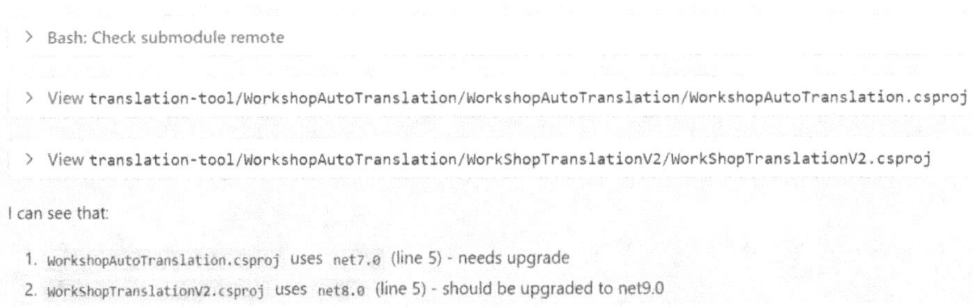

```
>  Bash: Check submodule remote

>  View translation-tool/WorkshopAutoTranslation/WorkshopAutoTranslation/WorkshopAutoTranslation.csproj

>  View translation-tool/WorkshopAutoTranslation/WorkShopTranslationV2/WorkShopTranslationV2.csproj
```

I can see that:

1. `WorkshopAutoTranslation.csproj` uses `net7.0` (line 5) - needs upgrade
2. `WorkShopTranslationV2.csproj` uses `net8.0` (line 5) - should be upgraded to net9.0

Figure 5-26. *Copilot detected list of projects to be updated*

Copilot has finally finished upgrading all the .NET projects to target framework 9.0 in the new commit and verified whether projects compiled successfully after the upgrade. Figure 5-27 shows a newly added code comment created by Copilot on the Pull request, once the task was completed.

Figure 5-27. Copilot added message about upgrading projects to .NET 9.0

Using the **"Add your review"** button, you can cross verify the output from Copilot before approving the pull request. If needed, you can also add more comments for Copilot to iterate on the comments. Once you are satisfied with the outcome and get necessary approvals, you can go ahead and merge the pull request.

Demonstration 4

In this demonstration, we will assign an existing GitHub Issue to GitHub Copilot Coding Agent and observe how the magic unfolds.

We will leverage the same issue that we created in demonstration 1 and assign it to Copilot on Github.com, as shown in Figure 5-28.

Figure 5-28. Shows "Assign to Copilot" option available on the GitHub Issue

Once you click on "Assign to Copilot" button on the issue, a new popup window will appear as shown in Figure 5-29.

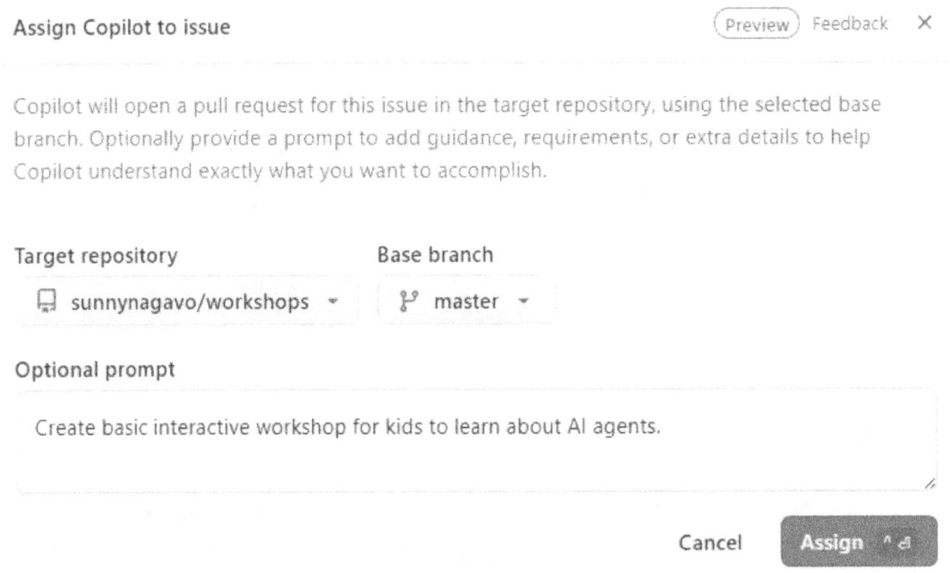

Figure 5-29. Displays "Assign Copilot to Issue" confirmation window

You can select the target repository and branch and provide optional prompts to add more instructions to copilot before clicking "Assign" button.

Copilot immediately linked a Work in progress [WIP] Pull request to this issue as shown in Figure 5-30.

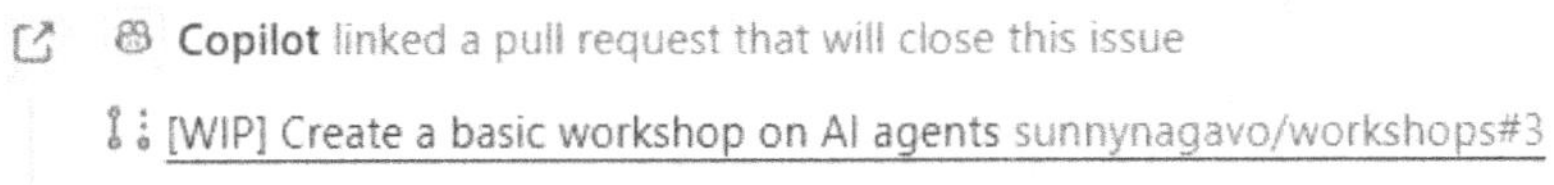

Figure 5-30. Copilot linked draft WIP pull request to the issue

Like Demonstration 3, you can click on "view session" to see more details. In the PR conversation, Coding Agent created multiple tasks as it's a multistep activity which it will work on it and update the PR accordingly as shown in Figure 5-31.

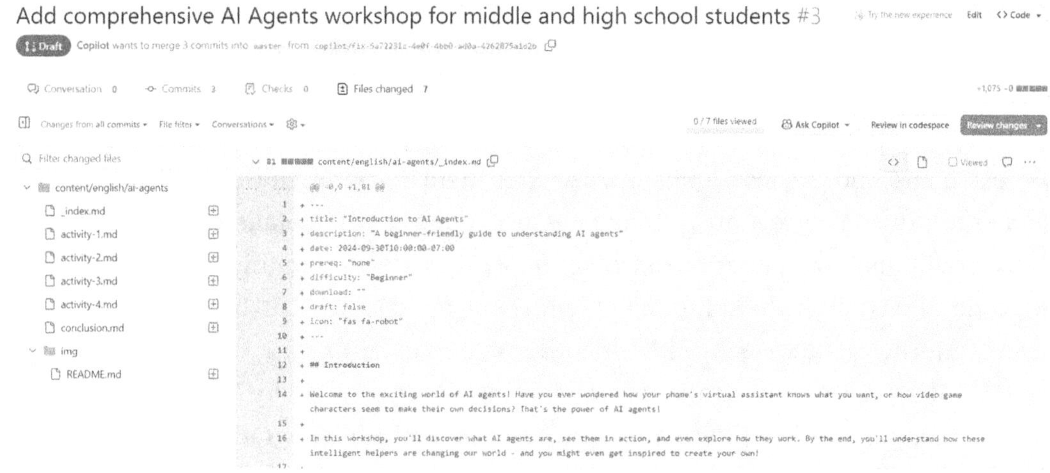

Figure 5-31. *GitHub Copilot has created multiple tasks in the Pull request conversation*

After a few minutes, GitHub Copilot Coding Agent finished updating the PR and the outcome shows the interactive workshop created from scratch by adding appropriate files explaining about AI agents, as shown in Figure 5-32.

Figure 5-32. *Displays completed Pull request with the list of files added to it*

Note that the PR title got updated and copilot removed [WIP] from the title. As an author, you need to verify the AI-generated files and workshop activities and provide comments for Copilot to work on it. You can request code review approvals from your team and once you get it, you can go ahead and merge the pull request into the master branch.

Q&A Session

Q5.1 What is MCP and why is it important for AI development?

MCP stands for Model context protocol, which is an open source standard protocol created by Anthropic that standardized the way Large Language Models (LLMs) interact with external systems and data sources.

Q5.2 What are the three main capabilities that MCP servers can expose?

MCP servers can expose three types of capabilities: 1) **Tools** - functions that LLMs can call to perform specific actions like database operations or API calls; 2) **Resources** – data sources that LLMs can access for information like files or database records; and 3) **Prompts** – Predefined templates that optimize interactions with LLMs through variable substitutions.

Q5.3 What are the two ways to configure GitHub MCP server?

You can configure GitHub MCP server as either Local or Remote. For more details about how to set up, refer to GitHub MCP server section.

Q5.4 How does GitHub Copilot Coding Agent work differently than traditional AI assistants?

GitHub Copilot Coding Agent works autonomously on tasks by ingesting repository context, plans, and creates multisteps, executes them in a secured isolated environment, iterates to work on corrections, and creates pull requests with detailed documentation. Unlike traditional assistants, it can work independently across multiple files, write and test code, and compile the solution to identify any build issues. GitHub Copilot Coding Agent performs all these tasks without constant human guidance.

Q5.5 What are the two transport layer methods supported by MCP?

MCP supports STDIO (Standard Input/Output) for local integrations where both client and server reside in the same environment, and HTTP + SSE (Server-Sent Events) for remote connections where MCP server runs as a separate web service, using HTTP for client requests and SSE for real-time server responses and streaming.

Summary

In this chapter, we explored the importance of Model Context Protocol (MCP) and how we can leverage GitHub MCP server and its tools and functionalities right within Visual Studio using MCP client (GitHub Copilot). We explored the security concerns about MCP protocol and also explored how to create a brand-new MCP server using C# in no time. Finally, we ended the chapter by exploring GitHub Coding agents and how to leverage it for performing coding tasks directly on the GitHub Web interface. By leveraging GitHub Coding agents, we will witness significant boost in the developer productivity; however, the onus will be on the author who assigned the task to coding agent, to make sure the generated code is in fact doing the right thing with no regressions.

In the next chapter, we will explore new feature releases from GitHub Copilot. It's hard to keep up with the pace of GitHub Copilot as the team is releasing features at a rapid pace and a bunch of new features were released right during the production edits of this book. I am glad to incorporate as many new features as possible in Chapter 6, so do not skip it.

Exploring New Features from GitHub Copilot

In Chapter 5, we looked into advanced features of GitHub Copilot like Model Context Protocol (MCP) and GitHub Copilot Coding Agents. In this chapter, we will look at some of the recently released new features from GitHub Copilot. It is difficult to keep track of all the newly released features and the rate at which these features are being released is unbelievable. Yet I have captured some of the important features to discuss including revolutionary GitHub CLI and GitHub Spark platform for building applications. The learning objectives for this chapter include the following:

- Exploring GitHub Copilot Command Line Interface (CLI)

- Discover Auto mode inside GitHub Copilot model selection.

- GitHub Spark, a revolutionary web interface for creating end-to-end solutions

- Leveraging GitHub Copilot during debugging mode

- Fixing compilation errors by interacting with Copilot directly from errors window

GitHub Copilot CLI

GitHub CLI (Command Line Interface) extends GitHub Copilot's capabilities beyond the IDE, allowing developers to interact with AI assistance directly from the terminal. GitHub Copilot extension for GitHub CLI has been deprecated and has been replaced by the new GitHub Copilot CLI. It is currently supported on Linux, MacOS, and windows from within WSL (windows subsystem for Linux) and native support in PowerShell (above v6) is available.

© Naga Santhosh Reddy Vootukuri 2025
N. S. Reddy Vootukuri, *Vibe Coding with GitHub Copilot*, https://doi.org/10.1007/979-8-8688-2196-7_6

Let's install GitHub Copilot CLI via PowerShell on a windows machine. Open PowerShell window and run the command below to install GitHub Copilot CLI globally with npm as shown in Figure 6-1.

```
npm install -g @github/copilot
```

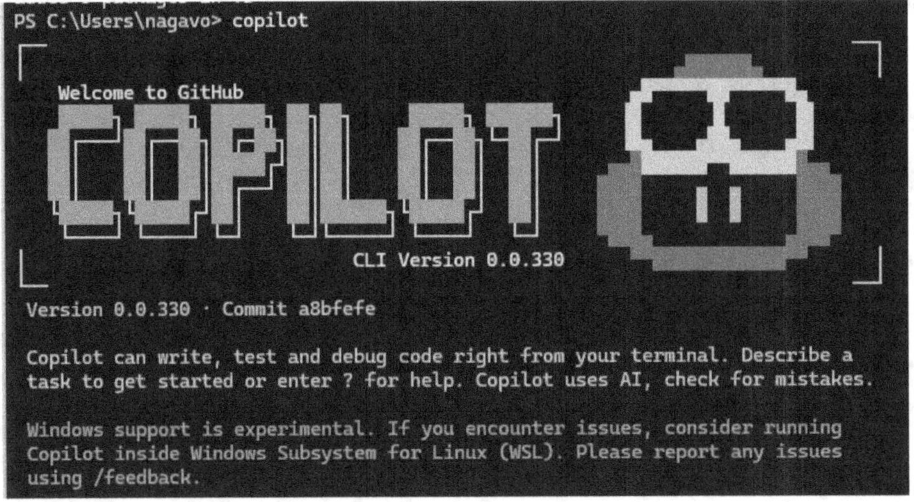

Figure 6-1. *npm install command added 5 new packages*

To launch Copilot CLI, type Copilot in the same PowerShell window as shown in Figure 6-2, which will display an adorable welcome banner image and provide a brief description of Copilot capabilities along with the version number.

Figure 6-2. *Launching Copilot inside PowerShell window*

Note   Windows support is experimental. If you encounter issues, consider running Copilot inside Windows Subsystem for Linux (WSL).

Copilot responds with a confirmation message asking users to grant permissions to trust files in the current folder so that Copilot may read those files in the folder as shown in Figure 6-3.

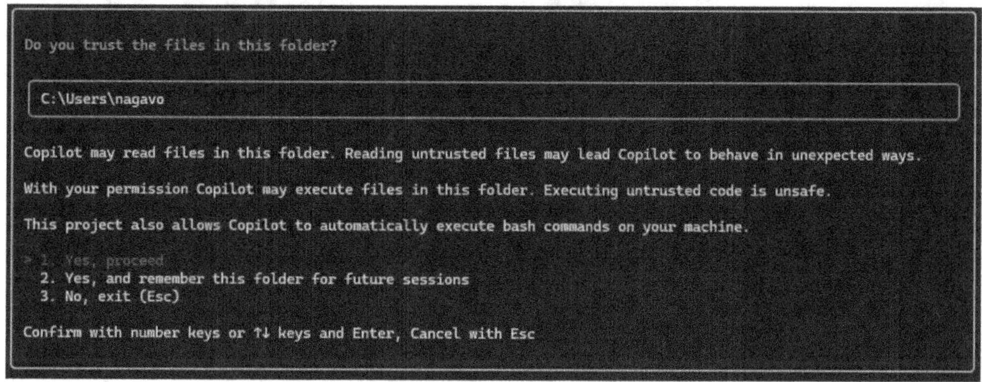

Figure 6-3. *Confirmation message to trust files in the folder*

If you are not currently logged in to GitHub, you need to prompt /login command to authenticate on a web browser as shown in Figure 6-4.

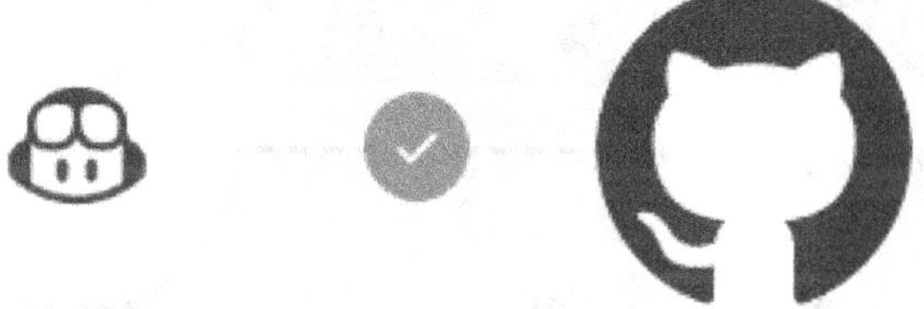

Figure 6-4. *Authorization confirmation message to give permission to GitHub Copilot CLI*

Once authorized, you will see a successfully signed in message as shown in Figure 6-5.

Figure 6-5. *Displays successfully logged in message from GitHub Copilot CLI*

Note   By default, Copilot utilizes "Claude-Sonnet-4" model.

You can run /model slash command to choose from available models including Claude Sonnet 4.5, GPT-5 as shown in Figure 6-6.

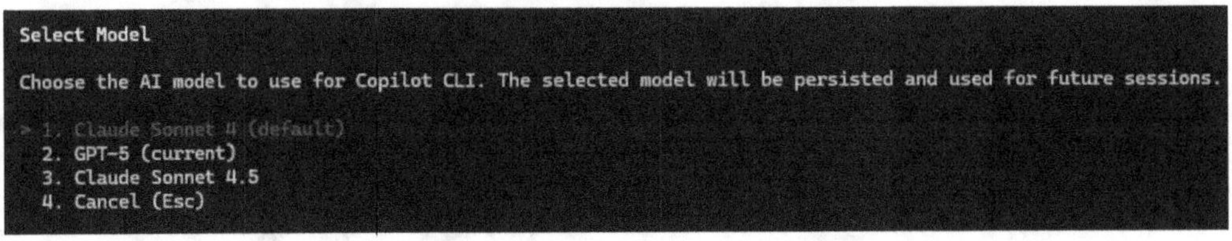

Figure 6-6. *Displays the list of available models to choose from*

Using GitHub Copilot CLI, you can perform almost all the tasks that you do with GitHub Copilot on Visual Studio. You can interact with GitHub to list open Pull requests or simply work on any open GitHub Issue.

New Models Available on GitHub Copilot

Two new models are released and available from GitHub Copilot on Visual Studio.

- Anthropic Claude Sonnet 4.5 is rolling out in GitHub Copilot to Pro, Pro+, Business, and Enterprise as shown in Figure 6-7.

- XAI Grok 4 is now available on Azure AI Foundry. It brings frontier-level performance with 128K context, first principles reasoning, and real-time insights. Microsoft safeguards are built in across prompts and deployment. By default, Azure AI Content Safety is on.

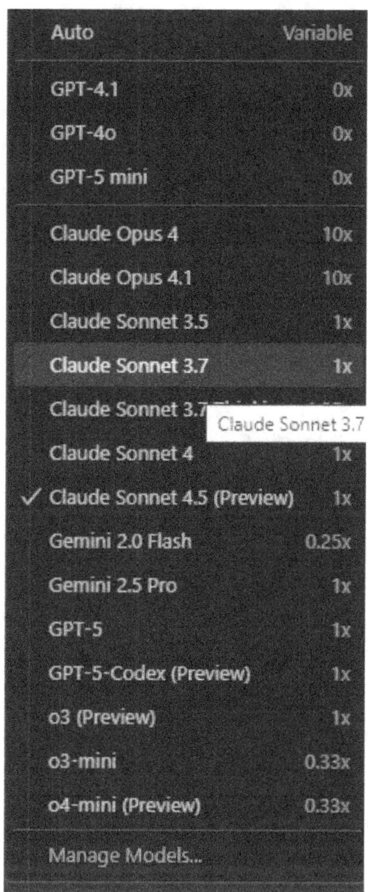

Figure 6-7. *Displays list of available models inside GitHub Copilot from Visual Studio code*

Auto Mode to Select Models

New Auto variable mode is available on the top section as shown in Figure 6-7, when selecting models in GitHub Copilot inside Visual Studio Code.

Auto Mode will pick from **GPT-4.1, GPT-5, GPT-5 mini, and Claude Sonnet 4**. If you pick Auto Mode, you can get a discount on the premium request (if one gets used) so it's like you're getting a free premium request with every 10 Auto mode uses.

GitHub Copilot Inside Debugging Mode

GitHub Copilot is added inside exception windows as shown in Figure 6-8, where Copilot can understand the context and work on it instead of manually copying the exception details to interact with GitHub Copilot.

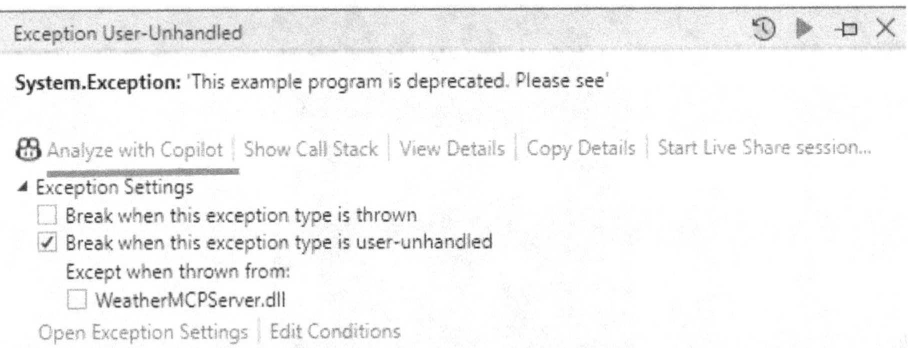

Figure 6-8. *Displays "Analyze with Copilot" option inside exceptions dialog box*

Once you click on the Analyze option, a new Copilot chat window is opened as shown in Figure 6-9, where Copilot will analyze the issue and provide meaningful suggestions.

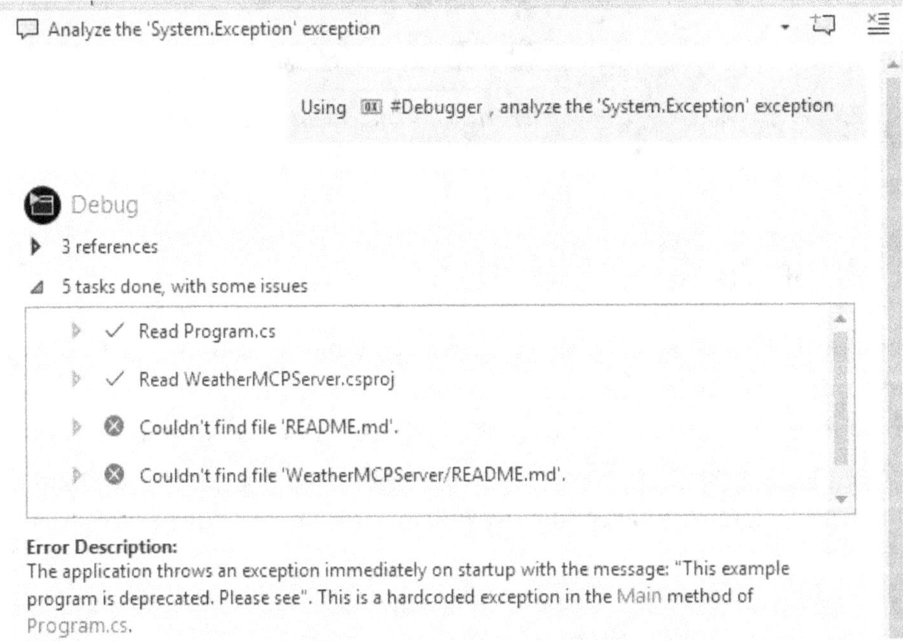

Figure 6-9. *Copilot message explaining about the exception message*

Notice, there is a new mode called "Debug" is now available in this thread as shown in Figure 6-10.

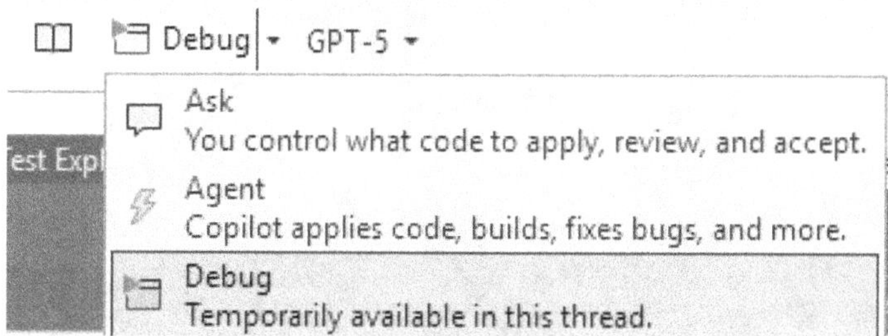

Figure 6-10. *Debug mode available temporarily in this thread*

GitHub Copilot Modernization Experience

On any dotnet project, right-click and select Modernize option as shown in Figure 6-11.

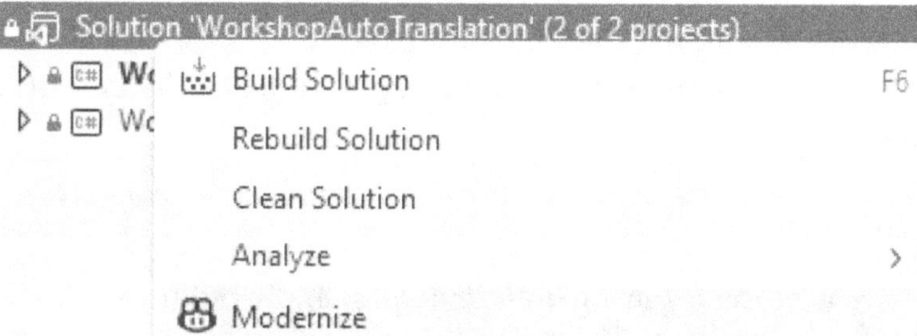

Figure 6-11. *Right-click on solution to display "Modernize" option inside popup window*

Once you select Modernize option, GitHub Copilot responds with a detailed response explaining about .NET App modernization experience as shown in Figure 6-12.

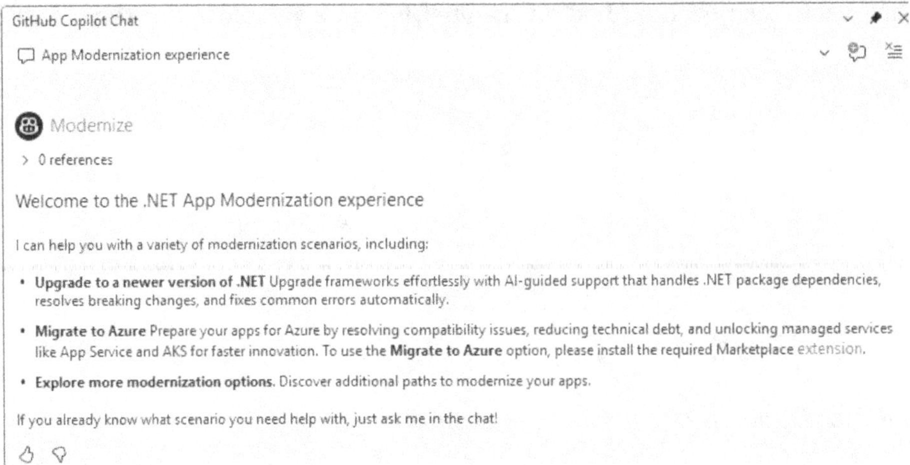

Figure 6-12. *Copilot response about .NET app modernization experience*

GitHub Spark for Creating End-to-End Solutions

GitHub team released Spark, which is in public preview for Copilot Pro+ subscribers. It's a revolutionary platform where GitHub Spark takes your ideas via prompts to deployed applications in minutes.

Sign up for a Pro+ account using the link `https://github.com/github-spark/pro-plus` to access Spark.

Once you have access, navigate to github.com/spark to build your first application using GitHub Spark as shown in Figure 6-13.

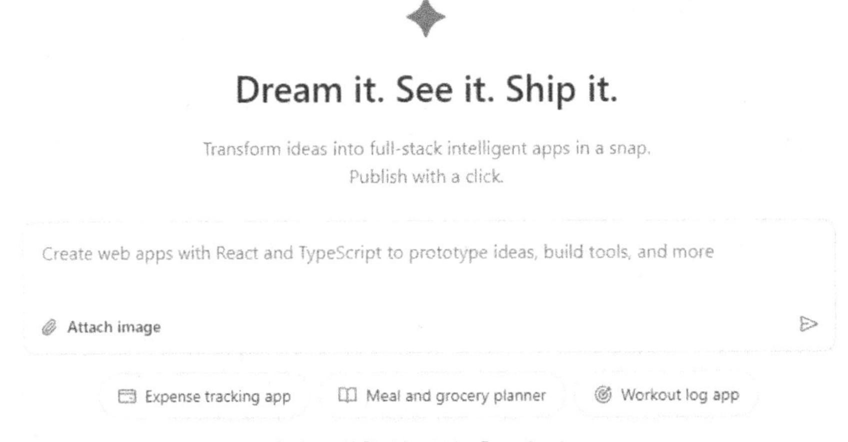

Figure 6-13. *Home page of GitHub Spark Web interface*

As mentioned, you can transform your ideas into a full-stack intelligent application and publish it to cloud within no time.

Demonstration 1

In this demonstration, let's use GitHub Spark to create a tic tac toe game with rich colors.

Prompt: Create a tic tac toe game with rich colors and use traditional X and O.

GitHub Spark started thinking and working on generating code for my tic tac toe application as shown in Figure 6-14.

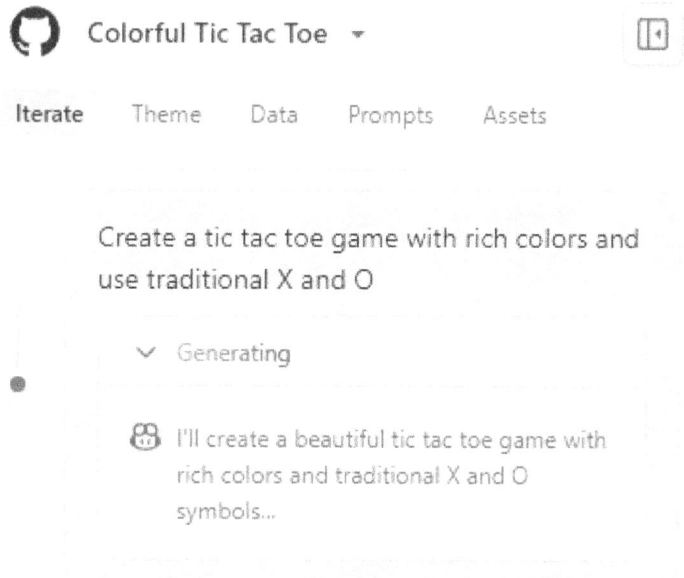

Figure 6-14. *GitHub Spark working on the game based on user prompt*

GitHub Spark went ahead, and generated PRD (product requirements document) and necessary files as shown in Figure 6-15.

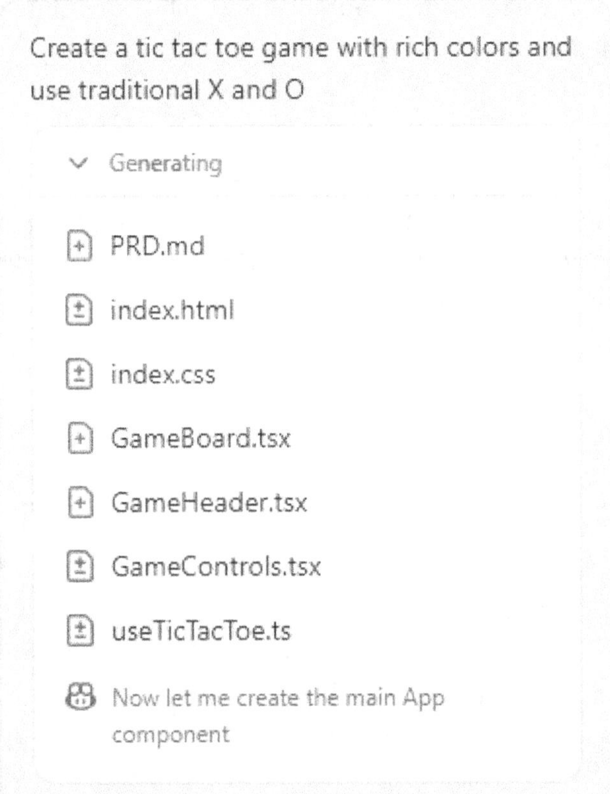

Figure 6-15. *GitHub Spark generating necessary files for the user prompt*

Once GitHub Spark completed working on the task, it created an adorable working application with rich user interface as shown in Figure 6-16. Notice, we didn't write a single line of code other than providing detailed user prompt.

Figure 6-16. *Tic Tac Toe application developed by GitHub Spark*

We can also publish this application using GitHub Spark. This revolutionary interface will help developers to quickly create prototypes to convert their ideas into working examples within no time.

Summary

In this chapter, we explored some of the newly released features. The rate at which the GitHub Copilot team is releasing features is unbelievable, and I suggest you keep track on the GitHub Copilot blog for the latest updates and announcements. If you have reached here, it means you thoroughly enjoyed reading this book as much as I did writing it. Keep practicing and using GitIIub Copilot in your daily coding tasks to appreciate the power of it. Happy coding!!

Index

I, J, K

L

M, N

O

P, Q

R

S, T

U

GPSR Compliance
The European Union's (EU) General Product Safety Regulation (GPSR) is a set
of rules that requires consumer products to be safe and our obligations to
ensure this.

If you have any concerns about our products, you can contact us on

ProductSafety@springernature.com

In case Publisher is established outside the EU, the EU authorized
representative is:

Springer Nature Customer Service Center GmbH
Europaplatz 3
69115 Heidelberg, Germany